Mingled Voices 5

International Proverse Poetry Prize Anthology 2020

Proverse Hong Kong

2021

Proverse Hong Kong fully supports freedom of artistic expression. The views and opinions expressed in this book are those of the individual writers over whose names the various texts appear, or which are otherwise attributed to them (for example in the 'Poets' Biographies' and /or 'Poets' Notes and Commentaries'), and do not represent the views and opinions of Proverse Hong Kong, the Editors, or any other writers or entities named in this book.

MINGLED VOICES 5 contains the work of ninety poets. The one hundred and sixty or so poems were selected from those entered for the International Proverse Poetry Prize in 2020, the fifth such annual international competition administered from Hong Kong.

The International Proverse Poetry Prize was jointly founded in 2016 by Dr Gillian Bickley and Dr Verner Bickley, MBE, in association with the annual international Proverse Prize for unpublished book-length fiction, non-fiction or poetry, submitted in English, which they also founded, in 2008.

Poems could be submitted on any subject or topic, chosen by each poet, or on the subject chosen for 2020 by the Administrators, "Hunger" (interpreted in any way each writer chose). There was a free choice of interpretation, form and style.

Included in the anthology are the poems that won the first, second, and third prizes. Selection to appear in the anthology was also awarded as a prize by the judges. This year, special mention is additionally made of three of these poets.

Poems were submitted from around the world by writers with a variety of previous writing experience.

Brief biographies of many of those whose work is represented in *Mingled Voices 5* are included in the anthology as well as authors' background notes on their work.

Supported by

Hong Kong Arts Development Council fully supports freedom of artistic expression. The views and opinions expressed in this project do not represent the stand of the Council.

MINGLED VOICES 5
INTERNATIONAL PROVERSE POETRY PRIZE
ANTHOLOGY 2020

Poets

Vinita Agrawal, Joy Al-Sofi, Shikha Bansal, Alan Bern,
Thea Biesheuvel, Liam Blackford, María Elena Blanco,
Gavin Bourke, Lawrence Bridges, Paul Brooke,
Lina Buividavičiūtė, Paola Caronni,
Vincent Casaregola, Anne Casey, Ian Chambers, Josie Chambers,
Krishna Chamling, Jessica Chan; Chan Kwan Ee, Tom;
KB Chan, Carol Flake Chapman, Cheng Tim Tim, Annie
Christain, William Leo Coakley, Suzanne Cottrell, Neil Douglas,
Gayathri Durairaj, Ahmed Elbeshlawy, Fetūolemoana Elisara,
Rayn Epremian, D. W. Evans, Adele Evershed, Ryan Fenton,
Daniela Fischerová, Lincoln Greenhaw, Casey Hampton,
Matthew Scott Harris, Kate Hawkins, Ho Ching Yee, Kathy Hoa,
Carrie Hooper, Joshua Ip, Kathy Jiang, Sadie Kaye, R. J. Keeler,
Lynda McKinney Lambert, Lee Ho Cheung, J.P. Linstroth,
Iris Litt, Sharon E. Ludan, K B Ryan Joshua Mahindapala,
Carmina Masoliver, Wayne Paul Mattingly, Jack Mayer,
Maya Mitova (Митова), Natalie Nera, Helen Oliver, Rena Ong,
Jun Pan, Danny Dylan Poon, Joanna Radwańska-Williams,
Coolimuttam Neelakandan Rajalakshmi, Colin Rampton,
kerry rawlinson, Melissa Reed, Vinni C. Relwani, Angelo Rizzi,
Halil Suat Saraç, José Manuel Sevilla,
Allegra Jostad Silberstein, Wesley Sims,
Hayley Solomon, Dong Sun, Robin Susanto,
Luisa Ternau, Edward A. Tiesse, Bibiana Tsang,
Roger Uren, Rod Usher, Peter Coe Verbica, Sarah Vetter,
Renee Wade, Victoria Walvis, Honghua Wang,
Bruce Arlen Wasserman, George Watt, Mocco Wollert,
Elizabeth (Libby) Wong, Wan-Ting (Joyce) Wu, Wing Chit Yung

Editors

Gillian Bickley · Verner Bickley

Proverse Hong Kong

Mingled Voices 5
International Proverse Poetry Prize Anthology 2020
edited by Gillian Bickley and Verner Bickley.
First published in Hong Kong by Proverse Hong Kong,
22 April 2021.
Hong Kong print-run. ISBN-13: 978-988-8492-24-4
Alternate (POD edition). ISBN-13: 978-988-8492-25-1
Ebook edition, ISBN-13: 978-988-8492-26-8

Distribution (Hong Kong and worldwide):
The Chinese University of Hong Kong Press,
The Chinese University of Hong Kong,
Shatin, New Territories, Hong Kong SAR.
E-mail: cup-bus@cuhk.edu.hk; Web: www.cup.cuhk.edu.hk
Distribution (United Kingdom)
Stephen Inman, Worcester, UK

Enquiries to:
Proverse Hong Kong, P.O. Box 259, Tung Chung Post Office,
Tung Chung, Lantau Island, NT, Hong Kong SAR, China.
E-mail: proverse@netvigator.com; Web: www.proversepublishing.com

Page design by Proverse Hong Kong.
Cover design by Pin-Key Design Co.
Printed in Hong Kong by Artist Hong Kong Company, Unit D3, G/F, Phase 3,
Kwun Tong Industrial Centre, 448-458 Kwun Tong Road,
Kowloon, Hong Kong.

British Library Cataloguing in Publication Data.
A catalogue record for this book is available
from the British Library.

MESSAGE FROM MARÍA ELENA BLANCO

**First-prize winner
International Proverse Poetry Prize 2019**

Poetry Is What Is Left Unscathed, Uncontaminated And Free In The World

On the occasion of the Proverse Spring Reception 2021 and the launching of the *Mingled Voices 5* Anthology, I would like to convey my renewed gratitude to Dr Verner Bickley and Dr Gillian Bickley of Proverse Hong Kong for the marvelous and important work they do for the promotion of literature, in particular poetry, and for the sake of independent culture and cultural exchange in general, both through the organization of the Proverse International Poetry Prizes and Proverse Publishing, which bring to light the work of many international writers who might otherwise remain unpublished or little known on a wider geographical scope.

I also would like to congratulate all the winners and finalists of the latest International Poetry Prizes in both its Single-Poem and Full-Length Book editions. Having been in the past the recipient of First, Second and Third places in the Single-Poem contest, I can attest to the joy such recognition has brought to me and, I am sure, brings to each and every winner. I therefore wish to encourage all Proverse friends and followers, present and potential, to actively participate in these exciting poetry contests and literary endeavours offered by the Proverse Prizes and Proverse Publishing. As writers or as readers, or both, you will enjoy and profit from the professionalism, generosity and warmth of the Proverse team aptly directed by Gillian and Verner, whose experience as writers, editors and publishers guarantee that your work will be treated with the utmost conscientiousness, love and care.

Poetry is a special state. I like to think that it is what is left unscathed, uncontaminated and free in this troubled world of ours.

I think of poetry as a state of language, perhaps close to the child's wonder and joy in uttering the first words or in learning the rhymes or songs poured out by a beloved voice, or to the anxious expectation of a youthful infatuation or a desired love encounter. But, above all, as a state of language which is far removed from any type of utilitarian or simple communication.

The type of communication that emanates from poetry, whatever its eventual recipient, is that of a vibration, a resonance, a tremor, a mystery, a complex, subtle, almost ineffable communication that transmits the distilled trace of desires, experiences, thoughts, readings, fantasies, observations, places or instants: fragments of life – of time and space – transformed into literature, or even myth, by means of writing.

From the writing process emerge texts in which present or virtual speakers or poetic subjects – that may be single or multiple, open or hidden – are deployed, and in which the reader can be exposed to alternative or parallel voices, ubiquity effects, simultaneity or synchronicity, intuitions of the void or the invisible: all forms of the significant vertigo of language. These texts are the raw material that makes up a poem as the result of an activity which is artisanal, differentiating, iconoclastic and uncompromising in nature, a kind of alchemy whose latent, enigmatic purpose is to recreate or reinvent the self, language and the world in each poem. Thus, each poem is, or can be, at once, a plunge into memory and the unconscious, a challenge to the limits of language, a dialogue with silence, a feast of imagination, an exercise in rhetoric, a duel with chance, but always a foray into the uncreated and a unique creation made up of desire and freedom.

I invite all those who have felt the call of poetry to heed that call and delve into its wonderful universe, as readers or incipient writers; and I urge full-fledged poets to continue to enrich the world poetic legacy in any and all languages, as beautifully demonstrated by the Proverse *Mingled Voices* anthologies.

María Elena Blanco
Las Cruces, Chile, January 30, 2021

ACKNOWLEDGEMENTS

All those at Proverse Hong Kong, administrators of the Proverse Poetry Prize (single poems), thank all those who entered for the 2020 competition, and warmly appreciate the helpful and willing participation in the editorial process of those whose poems were selected for this anthology.

We are most grateful, also, for the professionalism and dedication of the judges.

The Hotel Coma, Ordino, Principat d'Andorra, is warmly thanked for ongoing, always willing and friendly help with practicalities.

On this occasion, we give particular thanks to María Elena Blanco, first-prize winner of the Proverse Poetry Prize 2019, for her inspiring, accomplished and generous opening Message and to Jeff Streeter for his elegant and professional Preface.

NOTE FROM THE EDITORS
and Proverse Poetry Prize Administrators

For this, the fifth annual international Proverse Poetry Prize, poems were invited, either on the entrant's own choice of subject or theme, or on a subject selected by the Proverse Poetry Prize Administrators, "Hunger" (interpreted as each entrant might wish). Any form, style or genre could be used.

Poems were judged by the panel of judges as submitted and the following awards were made:

First Prize
Anne Casey, 'Night Traps'
Second Prize
Carol Flake Chapman, 'Sequestered Sunday'
Third Prizes
Jack Mayer, 'False Labour'
Maya Mitova (Митова), 'Notesheet from the Dawn of the Light'
Hayley Solomon, 'Tell me and I will Try'
George Watt, 'The Blackbirds of Cooper Place'

Special mention
KB Chan
Lynda McKinney Lambert
Natalie Nera

Several other entered poems were awarded a place in this International Proverse Poetry Prize Anthology 2020, *Mingled Voices 5*.
Their names appear in the Table of Contents as well as on the title page.

Congratulations to all!

Several of the poems in the Anthology were edited by the writers after selection for the Anthology and before publication, but no further judging of the entries was made at this stage.

All writers were invited to contribute a commentary and/or notes on their poems, to be included in this anthology, and have responded in different ways.

Brief biographies of those whose work is represented in *Mingled Voices 5* can be found towards the back of the anthology.

To the extent that those whose poetry is published here tell us about their occupations and/or working lives, we know that among them (the following description is not exhaustive) are authors and writers (including of ESL (English as a Second Language) materials, fantasy novels, musicals, non-fiction, screenplays), editors, essayists, journalists (including an Op-Ed writer and a former part-time columnist), literary critics, playwrights, poets, researchers, translators (including of Italian, Spanish, and poetry), a media communications director, former and retired librarians, teachers and retired teachers at different levels and for different groups in different areas, including American Film, Composition, Creative Writing, Environmental Literature, ESL, Fine Arts, Humanities, Interpretation, Languages (including Bulgarian, English, German, Italian and Romanian), Literature (including American, Bulgarian, English), Literary Theory, Rhetorical Studies, Linguistics (Slavic and English), Special Education, Theory of Knowledge, Translation, a doctor in general practice, a dentist, a former attorney, a former aircraft engineer, television presenters, filmmakers, a musician, an "occasional" blacksmith, a potter.

Again, to the extent that those who hold degrees make explicit mention of them (and not all do), we know that among them they hold degrees (including at Bachelor's, Master's and PhD levels) in, among others, Arabic Language, Culture and Literature, astrophysics, Computer Science, Computer Systems Management, creative writing, English and Linguistics, English Language and Literature, English Literature, English with an emphasis in Applied Language Studies, Fine Arts, German and vocal performance, International Relations, interpreting studies, Italian Language, Culture and Literature, Law, language and communication, Lithuanian philology and advertising, Lithuanian literature, Modern Drama Studies. One has a Certificate in Poetry. A few are still undergoing formal education.

One is an Honorman, U.S. Naval Submarine School. "SS" (Submarine Service) qualified. Vietnam Service Medal. Honorable Discharge.

Poems were submitted from Australia, Bulgaria, Canada, Chile, the Czech Republic, Hong Kong, India, Ireland, Macau, Nepal, New Zealand, Singapore, the Peoples' Republic of China, the United Kingdom, the United States of America, and Turkey.

The countries of birth of these poets include Australia, Bulgaria, Cuba, the Czech Republic, Egypt, Germany, Hong Kong, India, Indonesia, Ireland, Italy, Nepal, New Zealand, Poland, South Africa, Spain, the Netherlands, the Peoples' Republic of China, the Philippines, the United Kingdom, the United States of America, and Turkey.

Some are new or young writers. Others are already well-published as poets, whether in magazines and journals or in book form, some with several published poetry collections of their own. Some are prize-winning writers and/or winners of grants to support their literary work. Several have participated in national and international poetry festivals and other prestigious events. Some are leaders in that they have formed poetry writing and/or appreciation groups, including online writing communities. Others work in publishing or have their own press.

For at least thirty-seven of the poets, English is not their mother-tongue. Coincidentally, about thirty-seven are men and about fifty-one are women.

*

Entrants were asked to submit their work in English. To qualify, entries needed to be previously unpublished in English, but could have been previously published in another language.

Poems were invited in any genre, form, or style. Nearly all are in free verse; although one poet continues to demonstrate his interest in the figure six – six verses, six lines per verse and six syllables per line – and a small number use specific forms like the pantoum, haiku (and quasi-haiku), and acrostic. One poet uses a Welsh form, the gwawdodyn, and an Antarctic form, the zeitgeber. A few use rhyme. One work is presented in what one might call poetic prose.

Poetic techniques such as repetition, alliteration, assonance, lists, contrasts, extended metaphors, are used. The same poet who played on the name of the English seaside town

"Morecambe" in last year's collection gives us two more poems showing a similar turn of mind, this year being joined by another poet whose simple short word-play is similarly masterly. The imagery is apt, at times violent, at times loving. As in previous years, there is ebullient vocabulary, sophisticated and accomplished use of the run-on line. There are echoes from a biblical and classical education.

Perhaps most are written in the voice of the writer but some present a persona and/or compose in the form of a dramatic monologue. (The "back-stories" provided for many of the poems help us to know which are which.) Some seek to understand and present life and experiences from the perspective of others (human or other forms of life or existence).

As always, a wide range of subjects, situations, events, arguments, moods and emotions is displayed in the anthology as a whole.

The subject selected by the Proverse Poetry Prize Administrators – "Hunger" (interpreted as each writer might desire) – proved to be popular. Fifteen titles include the word, 'hunger' and the word occurs 130 times in the anthology as a whole. Related words occur as follows: eat (12 times), eating (9), food (54), hungry (33), starve (5), starving (2), crave (2), craving (2), oven (3), bread (10), rice (5), salad (7), apple(s) (3), drink (5), thirst (2), thirsty (1).

Not surprisingly, remembering that the entry period for submissions ran from 7 May to 30 June / 11 July (late entries), the Covid-19 pandemic features as a subject. The words 'pandemic' and 'Covid' occur 20 and 12 times respectively. Some poems relate the two subjects, hunger and Covid-19.

The hunger described is for food to eat, but also spiritual hunger; for roots and familiarity, companionship, loving intercourse, for a loved one dead or moved away; aesthetic hunger; hunger to be heard or known; a hungering belief in the eternal existence of the self.

One poem refers to cannibalism; in another the poet themselves is aggressively mentally devoured. In yet another, human compulsive eating is offered redemption by comparison with the compulsive eating of a caterpillar, which must eat to trigger the fulfillment of change.

Poems on self-chosen topics speak of personal experiences including mystic and spiritual events, the family and family relationships including parental and married love, rural and urban landscapes, events and people witnessed, political and geopolitical events, environmental concern.

A handful are ekphrastic in nature, inspired by other works of art – by other poems, by sculptures, by imagined paintings.

The moods range from nostalgia and sorrow to compassionate understanding, and admiration. One poet describes how his gift of heightened awareness of others is manifested. Just one or two give expression to humour.

Each poem was judged on its own merits and those selected for this anthology are arranged simply in alphabetical order of poets' surnames and (where more than one poem by a single poet is included) also by title (unless a different sequence was requested by the poet concerned). The poets' commentaries and notes on their poems, requested by the prize administrators during the editing process, are presented as endnotes. The brief biographies of the poets (which were not known to the judges at the time of judging) appear, as supplied by the poets themselves, in alphabetical order of surname.

*

All poets have shown considerable commitment to their participation in this anthology. At least a few faced more than usual difficulties in doing so. One apologised for taking a little while to respond to one editing enquiry, writing, "We had severe wildfires here in Oregon and I was forced to evacuate." Another explained that their delay was caused by being locked down in a place with no internet service.

We deeply appreciate the consideration and conscientiousness which has been demonstrated and wish everyone, their loved ones and families, a safe outcome from the present pandemic.

We very much hope that all who entered for the Proverse Poetry Prize 2020 and all who were awarded a place in *Mingled Voices 5: Proverse Poetry Prize Anthology 2020* will continue to enter their work in future years. We continue to welcome all those who entered for the Prize in 2016, 2017, 2018 and 2019 and all who were awarded a place in previous International Proverse Poetry Prize Anthologies, *Mingled Voices, Mingled Voices 2, Mingled Voices 3 and Mingled Voices 4.* It is a pleasure to recognize as repeat entrants the names of those who have entered before and to compare and contrast their current entry or entries with what we have seen before. We are also always pleased to see new names and we hope that there will be more new entrants in 2021 and beyond.

Receipt of entries for the 2021 competition begins on 7 May 2021 with 30 June 2021 as the deadline.

As in previous years, poets may enter poems either on a subject or theme of their own choice or on the theme suggested by the Administrators for 2021, 'Shielding', interpreted as each poet may wish. Full and updated details will usually be available on the Proverse website, proversepublishing.com.

In the meantime, we hope that those whose poems are included in the 2020 International Proverse Poetry Prize Anthology will enjoy seeing their and others' work and that all their readers will share the pleasure of the judges and the editors in these "Mingled Voices".

**Gillian Bickley, Verner Bickley
Hong Kong**

PREFACE BY JEFF STREETER

Poetry anthologies can come in many shapes and sizes and with very different purposes. Some – perhaps most famously Palgrave's *Golden Treasury* (first published 1861) – set out to establish the canon. They can evolve – as the Palgrave successfully did for around a hundred years. My own encounter with such an anthology at the tender age of fourteen was with John Wain's *Anthology of Modern Poetry*, first published in 1967. Dominated by white, mostly male writers from English-speaking countries, it nevertheless served as a wonderful starting point from which to explore modern, and even living writers (the first edition of *The Golden Treasury* excluded writers then alive). The current anthology, *Mingled Voices 5*, has, as I take it, a very different purpose, offering a snapshot of contemporary writing from around the world. The result is a wonderfully diverse range of voices, all of them new to me and some of them new to the writing of poetry itself.

Thematically, the editors sought to give some shape via the topic of "hunger", suggested for the competition on which the anthology is based. While many writers chose to write on that theme, others did not. Unsurprisingly, the Covid-19 pandemic of 2020 was the subject of several poems, as was, for writers based in, or concerned for, Hong Kong, the recent social unrest. However, I noted that the relationship between humans and our environment – and above all our depredation upon the latter – was an abiding concern to many.

Not least of those concerned with the environment was this year's worthy winning poem, 'Night Traps' by Anne Casey.

Casey gives us some stunning lines, such as these:

"trust crumbling like the dust of so many
cicada skins so eagerly
plucked from nearby she-oaks – spectral sentinels, those exoskeleton twins
left to witness the fading 'Please don't bulldoze this'   appeals
falling on deaf ears –

a whole forest nobody hears..."

The repeated /s/ sounds scatter into our hearing like the dust she alludes to, giving us a physical effect that somehow underlines the frustration of the journey from the "trust crumbling" to "nobody hears". This frustration and a sense of disillusionment are the dominant moods in the poem. In fact, illusion and disillusion do a lot of work here. We start the poem with a childhood illusion that the mother seems eager to rid her younger son of: "At twelve, he's too old to believe in monsters." Yet at the end of the poem, the monsters reappear – in human, planet-busting guise? – and the poet is tempted to shield him from them:
"wanting so much to/lie".

The anchoring of this litany of eco disasters in an everyday domestic scene heightens its power as well as giving it a satisfying (if discomforting) unity. This is a beautiful poem which merits numerous readings.

The runner-up poem, Carol Flake Chapman's elegant 'Sequestered Sunday', touches on nature, too, as well as on the pandemic and hunger – including the spiritual hunger that is reified by the Christian act of communion or Eucharist. I especially admire the lovely last lines:

"I watch the monarchs flutter down
Like tongues of flame of the Pentecost
Teaching us all the languages we need
To talk to the earth and to hear each other"

The image of the monarch butterflies is a beautiful one and the sound clusters of /l/, /n/ and /tch/ give this stanza unity and somehow suggest the flickering, flowing motion of the butterflies themselves.

Among the third prize winners, I particularly enjoyed 'The Blackbirds of Cooper Place' by George Watt, a poignant, well-observed elegy which reaches a hard-won, if tentative, resolution amidst a "baffling harmony" through answering its own question about who will care for the well-tended garden left behind by the departed: "I'll go and sweep the path". And Watt's harmonies put me in mind of the musician in Maya Mitova's lovely, meditative 'Notesheet from the Dawn of the Light' – a somewhat Yeatsian musician who is "trembling in the rhythm of an ancient melody" and "gazing into the curves of his infinities". Meanwhile, Jack Mayer in 'False Labour' escapes the "cacophony" but, like Mitova's musician, confronts universal forces, though in his case it's mostly through the optics of science that he faces the "immutable laws of gravity and light". A moving meditation on the blank fact of the inevitability of death, the poem makes clever use of the motif of the salamander which slithers into the poem "obeying vernal dictates" but which also brings its own mythological/historical associations with transformation and (survival of) fire, adding texture to the poem's main theme. And if Mayer's "false labour pains" make for a deeply unsettling moment, so too does Hayley Solomon suffer huge discomfort as she confronts the hunger of others in her heartfelt 'Tell me and I will try'. Like the previous two poems discussed, this one confronts the infinite; but here there is little comfort to be found: "I want to do more/yet more/is never/Enough./There will always be eyes/Hungering for a better life".

One of the joys of reading any anthology – or indeed any book of poems – is to come across striking imagery or phrases that amaze and dazzle us and seem destined to stay with us, enriching our minds for a long time to come. There are many such moments awaiting the reader of this volume and some of these examples come from among the poets who earned "special mentions" from the judges. Thus, I was struck by the energy and promise of these lines from KB Chan's 'You Made Me Feel Like A Magic Man':

"Last week , I caught sight of you
running along the long, long corridor of our estate
You ran for joy and excitement.
Or joy and excitement made you run?"

Similarly, the description of a person as "a mixed-media DNA painting" both startles and amuses in 'Portrait of a Virgo Girl' by Lynda McKinney Lambert. And one of the most arresting lines in the whole anthology is surely this from Natalie Nera's heartbreaking 'Windowpane': "Every day / her ghost sleeps on my pillow".

Elsewhere, in 'Boarding Up My Heart' I admired the way that J.P. Linstroth uses off rhyme and repetition to combine playfulness with plangency:

"I wrote letters home
No answer, alone
Letters home
No answer, alone
My mama promised she would write, alone
My thoughts racing as on a velodrome..."

And it is hard to resist a poem that begins: "Rabbits are born / to know what rabbits know" ('Cottontails' by Joanna Radwańska-Williams).

There are plenty more one could quote but the joy for the reader, I hope, will be discovering those gems for herself.

Jeff Streeter is Director of the British Council in Hong Kong. He is writing here in a personal capacity.

CONTENTS

POEMS

ADVANCE COMMENTARIES ON THE POEMS

"In **Mingled Voices 5,** poets from around the world, often mindful of the pandemic, share with us lyric eloquence, idiosyncrasy and urgency. These poets give dynamic voice to the soul and its response to forms of Hunger. With distinct histories and geographies, these varied voices invite our continuing discovery and conversation on the eternal themes of longing, mortality and freedom."

Marion Bethel
The Bahamas
Poet and Proverse Prizes Honorary Advisor

"Each poem in this lovely volume fords a telling paradox, giving presence to absence while filling yet not satiating its reader with a hunger for its lyrical pleasures. The poem by Anne Casey, 'Night Traps,' moves towards a child who finds terrifyingly palpable the desolation that will surely arrive if our species does not gather the reserve to nurture its limited inheritance. Carol Chapman conjures in her 'Sequestered Sunday' a "vision quest" that each of us must have experienced, in solitude, over the past troubling year. Jack Mayer in a poem, set in Vermont, near my home region, is able to discover hunger as a presence within a "salamander" governed by the "immutable laws of gravity and light." Maya Mitova in 'Notesheet from the Dawn of the Light' expresses the synchronicity of discovering in the ruin of an acropolis a musician playing in silence – a kind of ultimate paradox. If one is looking for the magical sparks that come from playing a game of solitaire with nothingness, *Mingled Voices Five* is a brilliantly selected collection."

Charles Lowe, PhD
Associate Professor\Associate Dean for Learning, Teaching, and Student Experience, Division of Humanities and Social Sciences, United International College, Zhuhai, China

The Walk of Hunger[1]

"Reduce the length of a dark age
if there is one."
    —Isaac Asimov

This pandemic says No
to work, to livelihood to
jobs
The labourer, daily wage earner
is out willed, outcast, outclassed
more afraid of hunger 2020 than of Covid 19.
He's forced to pack-up and flee homewards.
He doesn't know PPE from Hydroxychloroquine
ICUs from CCUs
lockdown from quarantine.
All he knows is the panic
and the distance in inches
to a heaven called home –
a village hundreds of miles away
from his urban forays
where an earthenware pot
keeps cool drinking water
millet breads go down well with
white butter and jaggery.
He knows the walk could kill him
but walk he must – bent, burdened, *hurt.*
The harsh summer sun, a mute patriarch.
Parle G biscuits in his cloth bag,
his tongue pinched with thirst.
As his footsteps enter twilight
he knows that this walk
is about another kind of hunger;
the hunger for roots and familiarity
a circle where he's at the core, not periphery.
He wants to forget forever the cruel bald ring
of perpetual want, disfavour, dearth.
He was never a human being there,
just an appendage.

This walk is for a sigh
of self sufficiency, sovereignty,
a dependence on *earth*
rather than on someone who
behaves like its lord.

*In April 2020 millions of migrant labourers were displaced from their jobs
because of the pandemic. They, along with their families walked hundreds of
miles to their respective villages. Hundreds perished on the way as the journey
proved too arduous.*

Vinita Agrawal

Sometimes A Poem Is[2]

A poem is a malleable thing
It can tickle like a feather
Insinuate inside your soul
Burn you up or
Even turn you cold

An arsonist that enters
Then leaves without a trace
Sometimes it's the rock
Sometimes the hard place

A poem is a long love song
or a short sweet siren's wail
A call to revolution
A cry inside a jail
A vision or illusion
The problem or solution

An expression of wonder
a warning
a hunger
a tool to touch what's real
Probe the truths that we all feel
Showing us secrets revealed in dreams

Sometimes it's a belly laugh
And sometimes
   – it's a scream

Joy Al-Sofi

Taking Liberties (with Random Pandemic Haiku-ish Hong Kong Thoughts) – 2020[3]

Year of Rat arrives
Nibble, scribble doors shut tight
Something's creeping out.

New SARS-CoV-2
Lockdown, masks – we're stuck inside
But not everywhere.

Insanity reigns
TV cheers fill empty stands
Bayern Munich wins!

Ice-caps melting?
BLM? – Not trending here.
Social distancing.

Moon eclipses sun
Peony petals fade and fall
Hundred flowers bloom.

June brings lightning strikes
Power out(r)age, darkness spreads
Rainstorm warning's Red.

Comes the fatal blow.
Hong Kong Sevens're cancelled.
Surely nothing's worse.

Birds shriek from treetops
Crouching tiger, hidden danger
Drives the whirlwind south.

Candlelight flickers
Fear spreads fast. Must wild geese fly
Never to return?

Joy Al-Sofi

Thoughts on Three Chinese poems – 2020 Hong Kong[4]

1.
After Su Shi

Pink clouds gather as icy winds blow south
Stars obscured by steaming jade platters
Like the night, this good life will swiftly end
Next year, will I see a moon this bright?

2.
After Li Bai

Exile most hurts the heart
Hong Kong, time is now for parting
July winds bring change, only bitterness remains
Branches once broken, can they be rejoined again?

3.
After Wang Wei

Far away as Mid-autumn comes
Thoughts fly home astride the moon
A single unlit lantern set afloat
A dark gap – drifting with the flowing stream.

Joy Al-Sofi

Never alone[5]

Never alone, never lonely, never forsaken,
a string of friends forever on display,
never short of parties or invitations,
the eternal grasshopper lost in a stack of hay.

A press of people, jingle, laughter,
surrounded day after day after day,
until thoughts are flotsam; mere echoes thereafter,
keeping imagination and intuition at bay.

Every hour, every minute spoken for,
an empty day is a loser's blight,
how do we measure ourselves up now,
if not through the steady stream of likes?

Riding the waves of virtual voices,
drowning in the cacophony of comments,
the mind flees from reason's house,
blurs the line between reality and pretence.

Solitude, the cuss word of the new age,
is like the haunting night to be feared
an endless void that engulfs, degrades
erasing you until you've disappeared.

But while you rush by all too quick,
shunning the pleasures of the solitary,
you forget the sound of your own pulse tick,
succumb to the crowds, play to the gallery.

The constant striving leaves you spent,
you sink deeper with every splash,
like a deadweight to the ocean's end,
the Self grows dim – it turns to ash.

Shikha Bansal

New city[6]

A new city, I try to pry open,
it folds its arms across its chest,
in a posture of resistance,
grimacing as I wear my bogus charms.
I search for a nook to wedge my tired feet,
before I continue my quest of acquaintance,
but there is not a crevice to be found,
in its implacable and smooth exterior.

Shikha Bansal

Rodin's *Ugolin* to Dante's *Ugolino*[7]

having children, yes,
but nothing prepares like hunger
for the unnumbering

now I am Ugolino
staying ahead of the teeth & jaws
of my children, my sons

so loud – if only
they had not been born
they would be safe

their wildness
always ends in tears wept with
or without exhaustion

I should have shared –
oh now they have died
I must eat them through

freezing hard skulls
I lie over their bodies
still here is not warmth

if, then I might soothe,
but since not, I shall chew
never digesting
them forever

Alan Bern

Give It Time[8]

Death slowly by starvation
Is almost impossible to achieve
Unless one is anorexic, or African
Since good intentions halt it
Just in time.

Living slowly with frustration
Is easier by comparison
When one is apathetic or European
Since determined people control it
Over time.

Rejecting one's innate dignity
Is almost easier by comparison
Unless one has an ancient philosophy
That cannot be unlearned
Just in time.

Living off world-wide charity
Is almost impossible to accept
When one is proud and struggling
But hunger eats up pride
Over time.

Thea Biesheuvel

Shades Of Hunger[9]

Our pantry has long been empty
providers pass our begging bowl
averting their eyes.
Soon our stomach ache wanes.
Rumbling replaces hunger pains.

Our land has long been barren.
Sun and rain have gone on leave.
No permission note.
Soon we will have blown away,
dry as dust, full of decay.

Our loves have come and gone.
Emotions have been put on hold.
Easy come and easy done.
Soon love will mean masturbation,
no warmth; no elation.

Our identity will lack a substance.
A sense of self will empty out.
No food; no colour in our world.
Soon we will be a transparent ghost,
the hunger that will ache the most.

Thea Biesheuvel

A steel vertical pole

A steel vertical pole
vaults from a sea of clouds
up through the atmosphere.
You are climbing the pole
and have been for some time.
Let go, and you will fall.

Strong winds buffet the pole
sending strong vibrations
echoing down its length.
At times, it rocks so hard
that you must stop climbing
and hold fast for safety.

Recently, your grip failed
and you dropped ninety feet
before catching a hold
and falling no further.
You paused to still your heart
then resumed your climbing.

The pole changes with time.
Once, it became a square,
edged by four sharp corners,
unfriendly to the hands
and making the ascent
much harder and slower.

Later, the pole widened
thicker than a tree trunk.
Your arms, hugged around it,
could not touch each other.
Slow as ice, you crawled up,
face pressed against the steel.

Looking towards the sky,
the pole goes forever;
its end cannot be seen.
You can stop for a while,
smell the wind, rain and steel,
but you must keep climbing.

Liam Blackford

Fire (Australia summer 2019)

I foresee a huge fire;
our largest on record.
It burns all through summer,
then a rainless winter.
Smoke drenches the country
and ash coats the oceans.

A fire superevent
can be known partially
but never as a whole.
My life amongst the fire
is not the same as yours;
nonetheless, we both burn.

I have ideations
of fires every year,
at catastrophic scale,
increasing in fury.
Time is a flat circle
soon to be ringed by fire.

Fire scorches the landscape
and decimates the truth.
It floods all horizons
and hides in our plain sight.
Each time the truth is said,
ten thousand deny it.

I foresee an event
where fire illuminates
our shame and inaction.
Ten thousand animals
dead in a wrecked wasteland,
decaying year on year.

Fire is our libido,
our rage and our death drive;
it exceeds all limits
and loves no better fuel
than our own inertia
and wilful ignorance.

Liam Blackford

Unusual Uses Of The Time Zone[10]

Sinking into slumber as when wide-eyed
the child's soul suddenly sneaked out and
flew up to the sky / only now it's the head
crashing in syncopated plunge / as in a coma /
comma-shaped / hopefully without full stop.
Stumble over shadows / switch off the lights
at hand / too lazy to draw curtains / will regret
it at dawn / but it might prove a good thing
in order to adjust the inner second hand. A
murmur stirs out there / indistinguishable /
secretive park-bench whispers / or some hellish
time-grinding machine / get closer: no one / not
a sound / just one more step and shut those blinds /
note in passing the electric juice of watts and
diodes / silicon and metal circuits / read by the
glare of photons / make plans. Think: better
move to the written / think: all this neuter space
is the unwritten / that to be written / and the yet-
to-be-written is worth nil before the final causes.
The glass sets a deceptive distance between
window and world / inside it's still safe haven /
lest the objects rebel / lest bugs and other vermin
creep in and settle / requiring self-defense at racket-
point / lest bats' secretions seep through / against
which there is nothing doing. / Remember being
dressed / get undressed / lights off anew and the
night / the hushed / livens up with the spectral
glow of vaio and mac / red and green apples and
mouses / pings and ding-dongs from cellphones /
pc's / tablets / capsules shouting from the pillbox /
as if they were warning that until further notice /
or no notice. Knowing / that this hour is nowhere /
that it is future legend and / already / the past of
nothingness. And yet / what a display of heuristic
zeal this curious use of the time zone / from
neither here nor there / both meridian and parallel /
utopian / living how, in what orbit. Think: not
living / transiting / a guessing game of where
or when / a leap oblivious of the consequences.

Daylight takes hold / the yet-to-be-written shrinks.
Seagulls mew over the high tide / inexorably /
again / the head falls. The afternoon shall be
another day or night or beach / or pure conjecture.

María Elena Blanco

Unremarkable[11]

Brought the cold in,
bled from the right ear.
Cold wet, ceramic floor tiles,
the last of the chalices.
What is the point of remembrance?
Evidence-based, proof of the past.

Romantic recollections of nothing.
Braved grave illness, quietly,
with daily abrasions, of the body,
from steel wool.
Crushed by the spikes,
slow murder by morphine,
not for resuscitation,
this time.

The hurt from a hurl,
with a long nail, through the boss.
Success has many parents,
phalanx, poleaxed.

Ran around the classroom,
as if it was a wrestling-ring,
aged under ten.
Reality-testing, in empty vacuums.

Stood alone together,
for an imaginary audience,
that arrived late.
Turned like sods,
a spruce plantation,
for imaginations.
Forever,
when all change has ceased,
unbeknownst to ourselves.
Would have arrived on a horse,
if it was allowed.

Falling gently, into a dried-up river,
the ending of life,
and the beginning of remembrance.
The roar of the buzz-saw,
dispersing streams of luminous metal,
into the evening twilight.

To tell the time,
by the light.
In a world of appearances,
taking precedence over realities.
The developing brain,
in anxious circumstances.

A black, charred skull,
operating with wires.
In between breaks for sedatives
and the harshest sounding laughter,
coming from the toilets.
Sweating under layers of aftershave,
stolen from a stepfather's bedroom,
from the heaviest air.
With an imaginary mirror,
reflecting stained white linen
and a mother on all fours.
Curtains still closed,
long past mid-day,
late-spring.

Before them,
or after them.
A self-fulfilling pattern,
since the earliest years, of the bed.

Knowing you'll never see someone again,
even if you wanted to.
Swarms of locusts vibrating,
inside his head,
heavily medicated.

The reaction of the silk net,
rebounding,
to everything.
Recorded and replayed,
even after death.
Had a gift for putting,
a negative spin,
on everything.
Chronically sleep-deprived,
all sound, competing noise,
mind full of moving eye-shots,
glazed.

Sat with both retinas detached,
misdiagnosed sadder,
than they actually are.
The sound of a dying heart,
on the way to a hospital ward.
Models, targets, actions
and neurological reactions.

Bleak moors,
skies without cranes.
Wind, white noise, homogenous maisonettes,
hundreds of chimney-pots,
in each estate.

A man and a dog in the distance,
spiritless suburban horizon,
the other side of the river.

Ducks in lakes,
in empty parks,
adjacent to terraced,
red-brick houses.
Spelling a death-knell,
for someone's opportunities.
Drowning more than swimming?

A man that did well,
twenty-five vehicles on the roads,
and fifteen stents in his heart.
Private streetlights.
A boat up the Thames,
self-published,
to sail just once.

All the rage,
simple as.
Inner restoration to meridians,
over standard deviations.
Time and a pendulum,
used to lording.
Talking from a height,
unknown to self.

Masked and faceless puppeteers,
invisible arms and hands.
A prison,
squinted from a council estate,
long since demolished.

The frustration of it all going over,
unable to keep up, dismissed
and punished at best.
On high-alert, since birth.

Shots fired into an empty
coal-bunker.
The last remaining embers,
inked into young forearms.
Said a trans-priest,
would fill The Pro-Cathedral,
every Sunday for mass.

Blind to the lie of the land,
forms of the body's ageing.
Memories of the day,
they screamed and cried,
in their hallway.

Catching dripping saliva and tears,
placing wet hands, on vinyl covered walls,
knowing how final it was.

Knowing it in school,
knowing it with friends.
Only one ticket needed,
to invite both parents.
Biting without provocation,
bloodied teeth, always irate.
Eyes rolled to heaven,
since that moment,
before the age of eleven.
A shrunken heart in a chest,
made smaller with dependence.
Never stopped between,
bouts of involuntary bruxism.

Slowing eventually,
knowing without knowing,
as children always do.
Messages unconsciously expressed,
triggered without gunpowder.
Loosening,
what constitutes crime,
over millenniums of time.
Stoics,
falling over cliffs,
not coming back,
ever again.

White-grey,
yellow-blue,
blue-yellow,
black.
Slow beginning,
slow-motion ending,
unremarkable.

Gavin Bourke

The Farmer That You Recommended[12]

Time has two names, then and thenn.
Then is the lovely meadow behind all of us
with horses and sparkling streams.
But thenn is the next footstep from then,
what happens next, the next action, consequence.
Then's thenn is this word, this breath,
that bird (while now is just after), same
as then when you think of all the inevitabilities.
I confused you on purpose when I talked
about then. Then is a straw dog that hid thenn –
then you know as my past, like a female
friend living close by whom you saw
at the vegetable truck, the farmer that you recommended,
my past as you expected it to be, your past too.
Then thenn. Which one are we talking about?
Vegetable then or thenn, the moment just
before now, inevitable as sexing each other
all afternoon when then becomes the million
heartbeats of thenn.

Lawrence Bridges

Gwsberys[13]
– a gwawdodyn, a Welsh form

He claimed not to have tasted or seen,
never savored tartness or touched green,
never snatched through thick pin cushions of pricks,
never sniffed pies, flans, sour cuisine.

Swore by *rhagfarn* and stuck by chokestone,
he was a withered stump, rotting alone.
Forest was too dark for his tastes, pockmarked
with black trees, which he had never known.

We left a cake and a jar of jam
hush hush on his stoop, hand-drawn diagram
to our secret spot, our gwsbery jackpot.
Would he savour? Think it a left sham?

Days passed. Found him in the sweet patch.
He wore long sleeves and pants; his hands scratched,
a happy grimace on his sticky face.
A bucket bursting with his striped catch.

Stepping from the thicket, he beamed, seemed
giddy, ready with newfound esteem.
Someone revealed bliss; it led him to this.
Comfort from discomfort, friends from fiends.

Enlightened, he was harvester, baker,
felt center in our hamlet and shaper
of community generosity.
Brought slices of pie to protesters.

Fought for the rights of the downtrodden.
Tended our community garden.
Told others to weed their gardens first, seed
love, keep eye out for good in bad men.

Paul Brooke

Winter of the Pandemic
*— a zeitgeber, an Antarctic form based on the
light cycles by month.*

Intense suffering cannot be measured,
nor calculated by exile, weather.
We are all meant to survive together.

Emperors congregate en masse, huddle.

Heat loss cut in half. More creche success.
One penguin matters to the cold excess.
Each male starves for many months in distress,

takes turns at facing outer hell; shuffles

his feet with egg secured like a tether;
faithfully preens each heretic feather.
Despite frore fear, he keeps his composure.
Sequestered on safe ice reduces exposure.

Paul Brooke

Apathy (the heaviness of the hand)[14]

I never thought that a person's hand could weigh so much.
But then, I've never seen a hand raising a revolver, or ready to slap
a face in betrayal. I've never seen one scattering soil over the grave
of a three-year-old, or caressing someone unloved, I haven't seen
one writing a last letter, or holding another, departing hand. So,
they say,
I don't have the right to gather such weight in my ulnar and radial
bones,
they say, I don't have the right to consider my carpal bones
immovable.
I know I must move these hands for the sake of those stuck in
their beds,
breaking out in pigmental blemishes, having lost everything,
or for those who lost their limbs to shrapnel, whose hands now
belong
to the eternal ecosystem. Splayed over the edge of the bed, on a
frayed
bedspread, despite my self-scoldings, arguments, ultimatums,
I can't even caress my child's head – my hand hangs heavy, for, it
seems,
as soon as I touch it, that same soil will fall on him as well. I
struggle
with myriad black forms, blood that won't flow into ten little
fingers,
but if I am called, if I need once more to hold on for the road, I
promise you
my hand, world – when darkness comes, we all must pay our dues.

Lina Buividavičiūtė
translated from Lithuanian by Rimas Užgiris

Not Getting the Nobel[15]

Today I'm sitting in front of my psychotherapist and crying in all
earnestness because I'm not getting the Nobel. Forget that – I
don't think
I'll even get the National Prize, I tell her how I want to stamp my
feet, shred
pictures with my nails, fall on the ground like a three-year-old
having a tantrum,
and I am that child not getting candy – little Lina, waiting once
more
for the results of the contest with Depeche Mode playing in my
mind because to lose
for her means not to be. My psychotherapist speaks to that little
Lina
and asks her how she would rate her home – it just hurt too much,
otherwise, nobody really noticed me – only on stage, only in the
limelight
was I able, for a bit, to be. Fuck off, little Lina, fuck off, all you
teachers
who encouraged me – I want another home. The psychotherapist
likes
this latest catchphrase. But I still really want to win that Nobel
Prize.

Lina Buividavičiūtė

Out in the World[16]
For Anthea and Leonardo

I left you both
under tall evergreen trees,
enveloping branches,
and soft blankets of velvety moss
that will keep you warm.

You'll feed on oxygen,
carbon dioxide,
exciting, intoxicating staples.

You'll learn from, work for
the world,
believe in Man, regardless, love
this battered Earth abused by all.

I left you in a foreign forest,
but from here to there
it's just other faces, names
languages and manners.
You step on my same underbrush,
sleep under the same black tent
with petals of white glow.

A sunbeam pierces the woods,
darts among us, travelling for
thousands of kilometres
through another time zone,
another slice of the globe,
at an hour that I keep on chasing so that
it ticks with mine,
even when your night rules my day
and sunrise and sunset mingle,
still dyed by the same big star
that will also and above all be yours.

Make it yours. –

Paola Caronni

Street

I have seen and know things
that you have not – listen,
and I will tell you the secret
that the street is a river,
a river that rises first
in high ground, in distant hills –
clean, aloof, cold –
but cascading downward,
with each falling step, becomes
more angry and chaotic
till roiling with pain,
it flows merciless and deadly
through the city.

I, myself, have seen a thousand,
at least, vanish into
the opaque surface –
just today, I saw a man stand,
or try to stand, for one moment,
then disappear, less than smoke,
less than stains
that scatter themselves,
darkness on darkness
against the stones,
a river of stones, scarred with lye,
marked with tar, and each one
with its own strange story.

Vincent Casaregola

Night Traps[17]

"At twelve, he's too old to believe   in monsters," I think as we huddle,
> faces swarming with swirling colours from his bedside
> lamp, medusas
undulating in watery obscurity, fear clouding his ordinary radiance
and my heart

a snared hummingbird: the unanswered question my bright-eyed
boy flounders around
> always in darkness – shut down to his daylight wonder:
> rushing   to greet
the leaf-tailed gecko (long-time resident behind our outdoor couch)
which recently produced

a tiny replica, the brush turkey tightrope-strutting   the length of
the fence, wide-eyed
> possums glinting from dusky branches as his teenage
> brother grumbles past
to sort trash   and practice his cynicism, "What's the point? My
teacher says they don't

get recycled anyway…"   trust crumbling like the dust of so many
cicada skins so eagerly
> plucked from nearby she-oaks – spectral   sentinels, those
> exoskeleton twins
left to witness the fading "Please don't bulldoze this"   appeals
falling on deaf ears –

a whole forest nobody hears   destined to be carted off in
mulching trucks under orders
> of our neighbour, the State Premier, who visited his school
> to shake hands
before writing off   our precious bushland – where once he
bobbed   bound to my heart,

cooing as we ducked a troupe of black cockatoos swooping
through, toddled to the counting
> of water dragons, ran to track that elusive rock   wallaby,
> raced to chase white tiger

moths; stopped to probe bandicoot droppings   (with a stick);
chewed over   the albino galah,

anaemic anomaly amidst its pink flock – all signed off to make way
for a new   motorway
          with its undercover proviso: a thirty-year "no public
          transport" clause – artificial
sweetener for behind-the-scenes dealers, while it seems around us
the whole world is burning

or drowning as we flail   against federal plans pledging certain
destruction to Earth's
          largest living structure – where at three he paddled off, lost
          in wonder
and each year since, we've gurgled together through butterfly
shoals, skirting bug   eyed

reef sharks, jump-scaring at feinting parrotfish, gaping through
fogging goggles at giant
          clams and   brain corals, where we swam shoulder-to-
          shoulder with an ancient turtle,
before bubbling back up to the surface like his   unanswerable
question, "Where will they go

Mum,   when all the trees are gone? And the reef?" A thousand
tiny wings skip a beat
          as I bend to kiss his pillowed cheek wanting so much   to
          lie
to him that the monsters scratching at his windows   aren't real.

Anne Casey

At Yeats' Grave[18]

Poet,
you have left your mark.
Your soft tread
did not pass unnoticed,
fame chiseled in stone,
cold and old like the earth
which we shall one day share,
my name, like yours, etched
for dim posterity;
modest remains of a modest life.
Yet one whose atoms are
no less noble, no less enduring,
nor any less the stuff of universe
than yours or those of kings
or things long extinct;
ashes to ashes,
dust to dust,
quarks to quarks.
But what of the soul:
identity, passion, reason –
those weightless things?
In that moment when your light
was finally extinguished,
did your very essence
simply vanish without residue?
If so, then in that far billion future
when the Earth evaporates and
the universe recycles the remnants
of the black and the white,
the faithful and the skeptical,
the fit and the failed, the
demented and the sane,
in unbiased measure –
what value then your dreams?

Ian Chambers

Ave Imperator

I am no stoic.
No Marcus Aurelius sits
here gazing empty
from this window
at the greening trees
and the nesting birds of Spring,
at farmers' fields with their
perfect ploughed symmetry
and fresh earth tones.
No, I am a selfish reveller
in the long fresh shadows
of the waking sun and the
bloody wine of a dying day.
The time will come when
I can no longer enjoy
these natural pleasures
nor any of mortal man.
Fear, regret and rage,
irrational and futile
though they may be,
march within me. We
all face an earthly end
and as Yeats eloquates,
how can I know that thereafter
I will have as good a thing
as I have lost? Caesar,
I who must die
cannot salute you.

Ian Chambers

Grandma's Dilemma[19]

How could you have done otherwise?
In such hard times one did what one must –
even sending your only son away.
That was the lot of people like you, like us.

In such hard times one did what one must,
harsh necessity trumping raw emotions.
That was the lot of people like you, like us.
Our kind was not born to glide.

Harsh necessity trumping raw emotions:
from an early age I learned that unhappy lesson.
Our kind was not born to glide:
small wonder my father was tough on us.

From an early age I learned the unhappy lesson
frozen in these sepia photographs.
Small wonder my father was tough on us.
Having children of my own now provides perspective.

Frozen in these sepia photographs,
your sad dilemma has continued to unfold.
Having children of my own now provides perspective
when contemplating life in an orphanage.

Your sad dilemma has continued to unfold
and I try to put myself in your shoes
when contemplating life in an orphanage,
incomprehensible though I find it.

I try to put myself in your shoes
when you sent my father away.
Incomprehensible though I find it,
how could you have done otherwise?

Ian Chambers

Hunger

I have been starved,
endured desperate longing.
I ache for the feast
spread before me.
I want to devour it,
to taste every part of it,
savoring the flavours
and feeling the warm
textures on my tongue.
You roll over and I slide
over the soft contours
of your nakedness and
up the gentle curve
of your back, matching
your outstretched arms.
Our fingers entwine and
I feel your thighs part.
We are together again.

Ian Chambers

Hunger[20]

We can feel it
Gnawing into you;
See it in your eyes
Grown wise too soon;
Touch it on your skin
Grown dry.

Your mouth shapes words
Full of emptiness.
You have tales to tell, but
No well-laid tables waiting
To welcome you.
We quicken our step.

We pass by.

Josie Chambers

Of, by and for the People?[21]

Slowly the beaches are emptying.
The green flags are still flying,
But look – there are no life guards –
No one is actually watching out for us.
Still, there's no sign of alien invaders,
Not yet….

The word is we need
A new democracy:
One that will suit us all;
One that will open eyes and ears,
Teach us to stand by each other
At last.

Let us go then,
You and I – try to make more friends?
Make amends? Let's listen –
Let's learn what being human
Means for other people,
Right now.

Josie Chambers

Confined to the Balcony

Conscious fellow humans that we are!
Four walls do not stop our mental pursuits
Though our corporeal bodies inside it inveigh.
Like in zoos, locked up souls

Stride here and there in the tiny squares of balconies –
Restless and frustrated, yelping and crying, angry and cursing
The circumstances, and kick against the face of time,
Then stumble the food-saved body down carelessly –
A boredom text in a nook of chambers exhausted by
The imposing power of unseen virulent disease, humans
Upon fellow humans and animals; states and societies
Upon their citizens and cultures within their domains.

But only our physiques lie down there, logs thinking
In the full flights across the continents with people, places
Like Wuhan, Lombardy, Madrid, and New York ..., fuselages
Active: eyes behold the most agonizing areas and scenes of
Requiems; hearts feel the most painful cries; skins, final
Telepathic touches; ears, the most heartrending pangs;
Legs headless; hands, the most endearing soothingly gratifying,
The fates of tragedies make hands in the foreheads as
Emotions and anger invalidated, and mind reviews, revises
Back and forth – the history of mankind and metaphysics,
Intends to hold all powers for curing of all ailments
To secure peace, harmony and progress in this green planet.

Krishna Chamling, Nepal

Corona Virus: Covid-19

Be careful with that harmful nerd, cannibal which
Lurking in your domains, ways and things of souvenirs,
Useful tools around you, family members and friends,
Anytime this pandemic, unfettered uncastrated wild beast
May pounce at us anywhere in worldwide-magnitude as this
Killjoy of our lives; an unseen enemy is on, travelling
Around the clock, across the globe by air, ferries on board,
May make overland trip by anything as a kill-life – a plague,
Deadly threat, dwelling in living to non-living things
In our surroundings; a terribly black force, but
We must have our weapons of Renaissance: fire, the light
Of knowledge about its attack, spreading the idea of safety
Measures – sanitation of health posts at home and
Abroad with determination; a war waging against it asap
To combat this brutally cruel, schizophrenic army of Covid-19
With our wisdom of knowledge must segregate, degenerate
Its capacity to close down its epidemic journey through
Preventing personal contacts at public spots, shebeens, saloons
And squares until our inventive hands and minds funded with
Necessary arms of tools in laboratories may discover panaceaic
Antidote to the horrific invasion of Corona Virus upon our
paradise.

Krishna Chamling, Nepal

Global Peace

Tiny huts in places in lands structured with
The pillars of spirit and emotions, walls; ages of
Toil, beams; flesh and blood, eves of roofs; sense of
Humanity and its courtyards; love and sisterhood, but
All these inherent virtues are onset of honor killing, and

Mankind's par norms: their voices are stifled with jaundiced
Ideologies, freedom; politically walled in, peace; Marry Celeste
Missing in the vast oceans of poverty, illiteracy, labour and its
Breath – human rights; Bermuda Triangle, power juggernauts
Mystified and the judiciary; attend justice's funeral procession.

Krishna Chamling, Nepal

Withdrawing Us[22]

the ghosts in our backseat
are sulking, like salty packets
perched on the tired leather
an innocent kick to my seat
arewethereyetarewethereyetarewethereyet

the ghosts pouting for some
radio now, some berceuse instead
of this uproar, some sun
instead of this downcast
arewethereyetarewethereyetarewethereyet

you interrupt this programme with the spotting of
tear gas in front of Sogo.

the ghosts rattle
while you dig a battled
helmet from your backpack
i suck on your screams
through these dummy lungs
arewethereyetarewethereyetarewethereyet

the smoke is nearer
now, dearer
do you pray for us
still there is no room for
ghosts! a smile blisters your mouth
arewethereyetarewethereyetarewethereyet

you open the car door.
tear up. tear it up.
the ghosts invisible in the smoke.

GO HOME

the city pressed face down into the asphalt.

Jessica Chan

Pickled Chicken's Feet[23]

The city I live in has stranger things called food:
Pickled chicken's feet;
Geese, if you want an upgrade, but still also feet;
or that of a pig boiled in darker liquid,
the ginger rids the smell
when eating more skin and more lard than meat.
Juicy bacon from the lips of a duck –
tongue, to be precise –
might stop your mouth from watering…
but why not a whole cow's feast?
A stew of liver, heart and lungs,
cold ox tongue again with sweet and sour sauce.

Around the corner a reptilian shop serves colder blood:
Snake stew, snake soup, snake heart
still beating, clinging to the side of a bowl.
They say it takes a man to stand the bitter taste.
They also say that snake tastes like chicken,
as they take a shot of the wine
poured from the jar
with chopped-up spines on display.

Then finally there are the smaller and stranger things:
half a piece of salted egg,
a lonely stalk of veg,
a clothesline of salted fish ready to be sucked,
and a lot, a lot of onions
with pickled chicken's feet, alongside
my own personal favourite: soy sauce with rice.

The city I live in has stranger things called food
but also sentient things
among non-sentient sort of things.

Chan Kwan Ee, Tom

You Made Me Feel Like A Magic Man

I saw children run in
corridors, hallways
football fields, basketball courts, rooftop gardens
forests, hills, beaches.

Mothers, usually not fathers
tried to stop them while
gasping, shouting, yelling
even scolding, miles behind.

Babies, children, teenagers ran off
ran up, ran down, ran around
ran away, eventually, to leave home.

Adults have long stopped running.
Mothers are handicapped by their high heels
fathers by their well-polished work shoes.
Society speeds them up, rushes them
but also slows them down, stops them
holds their eyes, feet, heart, soul, mind
all of them, in chains.

Didn't Marx remind us of that long ago?

Last week , I caught sight of you
running along the long, long corridor of our estate
You ran for joy and excitement.
Or joy and excitement made you run?

Or you ran to lose your Marxian chains.

For a brief moment
you became a wild child.
You made me feel like a magic man.
As you ran
I also ran, inside me.

K. B. Chan

Sequestered Sunday[24]

Let's imagine we are on a vigil
Or even better a vision quest
Away from the usual comforts
That satisfy our many appetites

Let's allow ourselves to be hungry
For once and not sate ourselves
And let's see what we hunger for
Let's see what our souls are craving
What they've long been starving for

Could it be this quiet solitude
So quiet here I can hear the trees
Thinking out loud through their roots
So quiet I think I can hear wolves
Somewhere in the distance howling
At the moon that we can finally see
Waxing and waning in clear night skies

With no business as usual to interrupt
This new sacred communion we may drink
A heady new wine and break open the loaves
That miraculously multiply to fill us all

I watch the monarchs flutter down
Like tongues of flame of the Pentecost
Teaching us all the languages we need
To talk to the earth and to hear each other

Carol Flake Chapman

Gnaw[25]

My city's a child's skull full of erupting adult teeth, primary teeth
cramming into a crooked mouthful unsteady in dreams.
How did we survive the distance between rooftops and ground
over a decade, then decades without knowing how
many dotted lines have cut through the damp air.
We gnaw at things we find lately, numbers always etched
on slabs small, unnamed, in the rowdy green of Sandy Ridge.
We never knew how hard-hitting our jaws could be until we
bit into our own tongue, starved for another. Sometimes
it's a mute understanding of words, of rules not transparent at all.

Cheng Tim Tim

Now That You're Well Fed In Love

"Mr. Hall remembered one shady [waterbed] seller whose product
line included 'orgy butter' and fake theological doctoral degrees."
    —"The Squishiest Sweetest Sleep." *The New York Times*,
                                   Penelope Green.

A man arrived selling vinyl bladders and offering master classes in
architecture and design. "The way you can hold someone while
eliminating all the spaces is worth any price," he said.

I lie there. Parents call out my name, but not my parents I now
know. Moses and the river. Waterfalls are portals. Where I've been
fortifying. I'm in the experiment holding water's memory.

I know all you feel is his body and soft pockets cradling your joints,
but look around at where the mud once reached and dried around
what we now call basements.

I heard him tell you, "The dirt divines our future through the
windows' cracks."

When he's done mocking the waters above the electromagnetic
firmament, you'll remember how the storytellers used serpents and
wolves to depict wipe-out fireballs splitting open the sky.

I'm looking for a friend who loves me.

I have a float bag covered in velvet, thousands of thermal images
of original walkways leading to original first floors of mid-19th
century houses, no sweat, a hose.

There's a Chinese ghost city, an exact replica of Paris, built without
current people in mind, ready to accommodate 2.1 million people.
There's a liquid-filled barrier that's punctured every 200 years.[26]

I'm a manufacturer of starbursts in a plane of sensory deprivation,
a seer of what's been told;
I'll have you where the sky-rivers aren't meant to land.
Annie Christain

An Immovable Feast[27]

Ah, the roofs! the chimneys!
I sit at my window, taut
in the sexual delight
of all that tile and slate. The men?
The men are everywhere. I watch them work at the stone,
drive back the blackness: we shall return to the old
sand splendor – let the king come home.

In the gutter, before the Academy,
a man and a woman, as black as Paris,
are locked together;
they take their warmth and their rags
for what they are, their warmth and their rags –
I have so much love for them
I leave them to starve on their love.

William Leo Coakley

Ashes[28]

We kept her ashes in a vase of the Song Dynasty,
surrounding her with the flowers of April she loved.
It was set on the mantel's top, above the fire,
and when in despair we shook it gently,
to her something like music, a voice trying to console us.
In the morning the first rays of the sun welcomed her
but at dusk with the dankness descending
she disappeared into the shadows, as if she would never return.
At night we sat and talked of her, the logs burning,
the blossoms alive in the dancing breeze of the flames.
When visitors came who had never known her,
we asked them to imagine her a lady at the court of Shenzong
who had lived for pleasure,
who was loved too much,
who died in the Spring of her beauty.

William Leo Coakley

Cast Iron Mother[29]

The widow slings an infant on her left hip while
older children cling to her dress, they plod
through California beet and cotton fields;
she shields eyes from setting suns.
She rubs her lower back, wraps her raw hands.

Like her, like Florence Owen Thompson,
"The Migrant Mother," you wear tattered clothes.
Dirt cakes in wrinkles; muscles and joints ache.
Twisting your hair between your fingers,
you hang your head and sigh.

A single parent, you balance trays,
scrub floors, restock shelves. You clutch
the steering wheel of your safe haven
as you gape at appliance cardboard dwellings
under Atlanta's Jackson Street Bridge.

You stand with swollen feet in long
unemployment and soup kitchen lines
with your children, your baby birds,
crying to be fed, tugging at your jeans.
You bend down, stroke their heads, hushhh.

Suzanne Cottrell

Breakfast Buffet[30]

The choice of an egg –
fried, boiled, scrambled, Benedict –
is never simple.

She pauses, decides
if he is sunny side up
or over easy.

Neil Douglas

Chalybeate Spring[31]

In leap years this water makes the fat lean,
In years more ordinary makes the lean fat,
Kills flatworms in the belly, salves the spleen,
Loosens the body's clammy humours that
Threaten to drown the over-moistened brain
With sulphurous vapours which are, in the main,
Noxious to most of us gathered, anxious,
Fidgeting at the pool's edge.
                              Capricious,
We wait our turn, thirsty for the precious
Brown liquid dispensed by a copper spoon;
Tasting not sweet or bitter but ferrous,
As we kneel to Selene of the algal moon,
For this water to soften our sadness,
Cast light for shadow, make good our madness.

Neil Douglas

Man-made Shirt[32]

born polyester
35% cotton voile on my mother's side

her colouring
tones of blue woven with silver thread

his 3-button cuffs long pointed collar
Dacron swagger

slim-fit skin-tight
I loiter on a steel hanger

him unbuttoned
her longing for the body's touch

Neil Douglas

Suburban Crescent[33]

moon slides
down a lamp post
to the pavement, parts the hedge,
scales pebble dash, twitches the blind
behind her reflection in a window, breathes
a slow arc across the pane beneath the eaves;
ignores the mirror, its back turned away from her;
traverses mahogany dresser, wicker basket, bed; inhales
the linen – bergamot on cotton, tomorrow's laundry, Guilty by
Gucci;
shadows pillows tossed aside on varnished floorboards;
calendars the irregular pulse of sweet nothings,
rhythms, cycles; silvers breasts, torso,
buttocks, rumples sheets,
glistens limbs; watches
as her spring tide pulls
bodies together,
to ebb apart.

Neil Douglas

The Bus[34]

He insisted they made no difference –
the red pills, the yellow pills, my prescribed potions,
although he took them religiously, consulted frequently.
Then, drawing me aside like a fellow conspirator
whispered in my good ear he knew
the exact date he would die.
He knew because he believed in Fate,
felt it in his bones, his marrow, in his water;
trusted the voices
that spoke to him from beyond the veil.

ʊ

A bank holiday in August – a melting choc ice of a day
and me dipping my toes on Camber Sands;
the sands escaping from under my feet
with the gentle ebb, the lap of waves
and he upped and popped his clogs;
no due warning, no statutory notice,
before the due date of his demise.
And I pondered that sometimes,
on rare occasion, when least expected, the bus does arrive
a few minutes before the timetabled hour.

Neil Douglas

the doctor is a ship's pilot[35]

there is a simple dignity a natural beauty in the tidal system of her
consultation the ebb and flow of patients the first the last breath all
the heartbeats in between their flotsam and jetsam salt of tears of
fears submerged surfaced floatation of symptoms navigation of
complaints to harbour a diagnosis in prognosis certainty of
uncertainty and the patients did I mention the patients? cry of gulls
silence of fish their sense and nonsense the untreatable the
unrepeatable swell smile of the sun tug of the moon we are married
to them in health and in sickness as the ripple breeze billows
unfolding folded generations in full sail passing out passing on in
sympathy to the life empathetic a compass of kindness in the span
of a surgery listening not hearing seeing not watching the stars in
their constellations by which we plot their course in the span of a
hand in the pulp of fingers a lightness firmness of touch our turn
at the wheel of being there being here for them for us

Neil Douglas

Water and Power[36]

Even if endless fire press the waves,
It's useless! No pause on a restless pace...
Strengthened by an ethical storm,
Disturbed by the breathless qualm.

Proximity to flames never scared it,
But Illusionary horizons gnaw it...
Fearsome lunar pulls of masqueraded waters
Shaking up innate geographical quarters

Tides splash on the grating docks,
Disfigured, sick around the rocks,
Changed beyond its personality,
Battling for a peculiar singularity.

The truth it is said is in suntanned sand,
As ripples sink and weakly disband.
Detritus and shells wash up on the inlet,
A residuum of struggle hard to suppress.

The free waters and free land may stay,
But broken in pieces or flayed,
Till the tidal waves slowly fade,
And free thoughts may be subject to change.

Gayathri Durairaj

Carcass on a Bed[37]

Beyond the wrinkles on your skin,
Old love, first love, new love,
Impossible love, imagined white dove,
Lies my eternal fall.

Beyond your pale ghostly figure,
Merciless eyes, and cruel goodbyes,
Lies you and my unappeasable ghosts –
The ghosts of moments I missed,

Of words I never said and lips I never kissed,
Of abandoned streets I still walk,
Of statements that put an end to talk,
Of intimate closed spaces I never saw,

Of turbulent life stages I never lived,
Of a carcass that kept me forever obsessed.
Beyond the wrinkles on your skin,
Ancient cove, mandate from above,

Inevitable course of legend and lore,
Lies my eye, to me, lies my 'I', beyond me,
Making love, unbelievable love,
To my unappeasable ghosts.

Ahmed Elbeshlawy

Grief[38]

There must be a connection
Between this body which collapses
Under the unbearable grief,
The indecipherable loss,
And that near perfection
Of the art of making love
Above the grave – the secret
Moan and the stolen kiss.

There must be a link
Between the tearful eye
Which neither sees nor blinks,
Drowning in a sea of memories,
And that lustful eye by which the 'I'
Destroys the decorum of tombs,
Wreaking havoc in black outfits
And trampling on sacred territories.

There must be some sort
Of pact between the mournful heart,
Bleeding over the stone,
Calling the inscribed name,
And the blood which rushes
Through that shameless zone
Of a body that grief can't tame,
O, shame! Shame! O, shame!

Ahmed Elbeshlawy

Wishing I Could YeLL For My Mother[39]

Doted-on men guzzling,
swirling, teetering,
needle scr scratching 45s
   as they d

        r

        o

        p

   from their stack
onto the jumpy turntable

          guitars out, chinka ching ching,
          slurring Engelbert, the Beatles,
          slurping food fed to them by my mother

          the brother-cousin's drunken eyes
          dart <left to right> to <left>
          like a child lolly shoplifter

            scanning for my fleeing shadow,
            desperate to be unseen behind curtains
            that betray my form

              everything in s l o w   motion,

              ... out-of-body viewing ...

              from the ceiling, from the walls,

              feeling peeled, stripped already

my nine-year-old whitened fists
tighten the blanket over the bridge
of my sniffling nose,
begging to be ~~wrong~~   as the door of the room, shared
                                        with my sleeping sister, opens
                            to laughter, song, and my mother
                            in a paraLLeL universe.

Fetūolemoana Elisara

Birds

Ruby and
blue frogs caught
in my throat like
the sister in the fairytale
who was rude to the old woman –
if I choked diamonds I'd be quieter,
but I want to talk to you
about how birds are cute and
what it's like in Florida
where the air is thick with poisons and
evaporating pools
and the canopy
hangs low and close while the sky
is higher than ever.
Dancing we're both
sweating, I don't
notice except
when your hand accidentally
brushes mine – I'm
not reading into it,
I know there's no book between us,
not even one
with frogs and diamonds,
but I like it.
You've got the voice of a siren and I
want to be eaten
want to see what you look like
on the inside
hear the song from within
but you can't fly and I can't sing –
are we complements,
or not even friends?

Rayn Epremian

Snacking

I sit on a rooftop somewhere strange
eating apricots and chocolate.

One of them is your body and the other is
your voice –
I subsist on one,
    live for the other.

        I don't know which is which.

And the fruit leather I bought
    from a Russian-speaking man in the City of Love
is the petrified form of my
    petrified inclination
        to love
        and to leave
for another country.

Rayn Epremian

Goodbye Stranger[40]

The dark side of the Green throws a thud over the trees
endorsed by the pop of a lamp imploding. The lane revs
hawking up, and spits out a cyclops car. Its solo beam flickers
scared. After its running comes a quiet that talks. Distress thickens

the colours of dusk. We take flight, honing on sound.
It leads where dread lives. The unlit lane pebbled like toad skin.
Not the pitman's side where trees give cherries freely,
the opposing verge, the thickets of the house of the lonely man.

Wire and thorn smelling of grass, turnips and manure.
Along laurel roots and brutal flowers, a dog whimpering
lying full length dopey, sprawled like some do before
a well-banked fire. Is it Bess? – Anderson's black mongrel bitch

low-stomached from all those litters the old man hugged
in hessian and taught to swim with stones in the Tyne.
Bess we call. *Bess!* Shooting hands to calm rapid, runny fur.
Hands up and down the uneven ridge of spine, gentle strokes along

the wrongness of bone. Night reflects a wetness, dwells
on the whiteness of her muzzle. *It's ok. It's ok. It's ok.*
More than sore, from everywhere she cannot name, fathom,
still she tries and a tail wags really slow.

She would kiss us thousand-fold, run miles to please us,
retrieve dumb wood, dive for fish if taught, or fetch pearls
if she'd a notion of them. But, some monster presses out
vitality, breath comes home in puppy pants milk hungry,

relearning blindness. We are not her pack. She is not alone.
Servile even unto death, she seeks to please: licks my hand
then stops doing everything. The unknown way, commandless,
it is and then it isn't. No biscuit or sooth noise promises

could keep her at heel for someone else to watch her gad away,
free of leash and child loss. Seeing her go we weep like bairns,
curse the feckless driver. Then fetch Anderson, stoic as rock,
to do what he must with sack and stone.

D. W. Evans

A Crown for All the 'Gone to China' Girls[41]

She's kept
beneath a jail
of bamboo washing poles
where white sheets undulate softly
'Give up!'

She's a
burnt offering for
rough men to savour. Her
feet earth bound – her soul's embers fly
away.

She's a
paper bark tree –
days peel off in sheets. Her
story laid down – rid in the shedding.
Sleep now.

She'll be
reborn each day
a hungry ghost – feasting
on durian scented air in
old streets.

They were
sheeted in snow –
plopped in hidden graves.
No elegy for nameless girls turned
from home.

Adele Evershed

capitalist hangover

jets of blue
at five guys

bodies stacked
near papa johns

cs gas dispersing aside
a shuttered swarovski

the unruly mob
of riot police
bathed in neon

a luxury brand
mrap

now idle an
impartial eye

hangs above
in led

confetti for the crowd

just do it

Ryan Fenton

electric road sitting out area[42]

in since-dead
ye si's
covid-infected
north point

i drag my hand
over chain link

later, i will tell students
poetry is about meaning
what you say

and meaning other
than what you say

and saying what
you don't mean

and every
iteration thereof

it's exactly
as it sounds
in silence

i wait for
one to ask
who i mean
when i say
my friend and

to ask
why i smirk
when i cite
a fellow scholar

or why i rely
on the ambiguity
of "they" or why i
believe anything
or who
          unlocked the door
or who
          flushed the toilet
or who
          hides in reflections
subtext
beyond perception

the lyric
means
one speaking
to no one

and dissolving
into transcript:

"this poem is pointless
unless you've read Brecht,
and I guarantee you haven't,

at least not
like I have."

Ryan Fenton

in defence of the graphic novel or comic book

image of man
alone
at party
thumbing a washer
warped

somehow comforted
by tender regret

image of police
on every corner
in every state

image of the
spiciest corner

of a subdivided
hot pot
flat

image of
the sound of
water falling

image of me
choosing to read
a newspaper

image of me
writing a line
in the bathroom

image of me
doing a line
in the bathroom

image of me
merely
in the bathroom

image of me
enjoying a sonnet

image of an overcapacity room
image of an awkward introduction
image of a racist compliment

image of being bored
of expats

and particularly
the state
of wisconsin

image of an image drifting
image of the definition of metaphor

image of hoping
to see you around
image of loneliness

image of me
not knowing where
a hinge pivots

finishing this beer
and going home

image of me sliding
the washer into my pocket

Ryan Fenton

Self-Portrait with the Mirror and the Moth[43]

Bare bones locked the house from the inside

The furniture is gone
Mere imprints of frames on the walls

Only one picture is left
But whose?
And who is she?
she?
there?

She is scared
She
The one in that picture

A hungry, confused moth sits on her lips

Daniela Fischerová
Translated from Czech by Natalie Nera

Preservation at Byblos[44]

Sea breaks through camera
on beach rock below
this ruined temple

     – now echo rebuilds in the heart
            wave's crumbling

We think sanctuary, think escape
but here old stone tries keeping
an image from a god

below a roof of broken sand – see this tomb rain carves
           one small crack engraves my eye

Lincoln Greenhaw

A Taste of Loneliness[45]

There is rain,
hurtling earthbound,
shiver how near it mirrors
relentless persistence for wet and down
gravity becoming without arrival,
is a kiss gauged by absence, our name
upon another's tongue like seawater and honey, shapes
beginning somewhere behind the navel before
the sun comes up. There is rain and more
beyond rain outside, the same
plunge like slick lathered horses
no matter if ears hear, what
mouths long to swallow at night.

Casey Hampton

Wearing facemasks doth dehumanise socialisation

Understandable... the sensible
(three ringed circuitous) logic
to trumpet necessity
each individual moost heed
bedecking, cloaking donning,
ludicrous interloper facial covering,
(I prefer sporting
latest custom made
invisible máscaras faciales),
when commingling amidst madding crowd,
nevertheless coronavirus (COVID-19)
makes laughingstock kickstarting
maniacal paranoid testing yapping
authoritarians blabber ceaselessly
bleak household pandemic
plagues (sear ring)
robust human specimen,
hence yours truly,
a feckless (gibbon) primate
breathes sigh of relief,
why? cuz he counts himself insignificant
absolute zero worth
versus microscopic prickly orb
aging long haired pencil neck geek
best beat hasty retreat
to his man cave
not necessarily avoiding microbial denizen,
yet any potential suffering
scouting out troubadour woefully
jackknifed inept hideaway.

Matthew Scott Harris

4 Knocks[46]

4 knocks, on a door to a girl with 'just a face',

3 knocks, a boy waits,

2 knocks, on a door that goes unopened,

1 knock, lost in the moment.

Kate Hawkins

I Do, Hunger For You[47]

I do, *hunger* for you,
In the light of yesterday,
That filters through,
Old photographs,

Of memories shared,
And a past now declared,
Over.

I do, *hunger* for you,
In truths that never were,

In stories that have other meanings now,
That our life together is,
Over.

I do, now *feel* full,
Of my own dreams,

Of a future that shall be,
In sickness and in health,
A wonderfully, adventurous life,

Without you.

Kate Hawkins

Artist Abstract[48]

I chose Hunger to be my Muse –
I lift her bare arms,
light as the last breath of winter.
I lift them carefully, and twist them behind her back into
a pose.

Her legs grow gnarled like branches, so I
cover them with frayed fabric,
dirty orange to bring out the colour
of her eyes:

sunken and hollow.
I try to bring them out,
and frame her face with matted clumps of hair –
(which gives her depth
and contours her cheekbones –
they grow deeper
and more striking).

Turning the other way, she gives me
Her other cheek, politely.
I linger over her expression, forehead creased over
Years of oppression.

I give her a hungry audience:
She commands their attention with her eyes,
to her naked bosom.
I let her do to them
as she wishes.

Ho Ching Yee

My Mind Is Hungry...[49]

My mind is all consuming
Eating my goals, dreams, hope
My future too...

It swallows me
Chews me up
Spits me out
Gobbles my motivation
"I CAN'T WIN"

Making me hate myself
"You'll never be good enough"

Whispering in my ear…
The doubts I have
At night it's the worst…
That's when it feeds…

CHOMP!

It makes me indulge in
selfishness, greed, and immorality

I can't win...I really can't
I scream!
But the only one there
Is the hungry beast ready to consume my dreams

"I HATE YOU!"
I cry out
No one can hear me though
I'm too far gone

There's not much of me left
It's devoured most of me
I'm wasting away…
Starved

Kathy Hoa

Life's Little Roads

Life's little roads
May seem long,
Feel rough,
And lead to places of discomfort,
But God gives us the strength
To travel them.

They provide opportunities
For growth and gratitude.
Life's little roads
Shape our character
One step at a time.

Carrie Hooper

Marsha the Martian Cat

I'm Marsha the Martian cat.
I fell to Earth with a splat!
I bumped my head, thought I was dead,
But no, I'm alive, look at that!

What are those two-legged creatures
Driving machines with four wheels?
What's that green stuff around me?
My, how funny it feels!

What are those giant round plants
Will funny-shaped protrusions?
What's that chatter I hear?
It sounds like utter confusion!

Will someone answer my questions?
Will anyone dare to draw near?
I will not hurt or destroy you.
You have nothing to fear.

Carrie Hooper

Poetry Is Pottery

Poetry is pottery.
We fashion the clay of our words
Into bowls and cups
From which readers
May eat and drink
The contents of our souls.

Carrie Hooper

the accusation of the banana bread[50]

not the listless scroll through feed, or swipe
through story. not the making lists or ticking
off. not the shelf-scour, the drawer-sweep,
the gathering of rare eggs, greasing a non-stick

pan. was never hands-on. baking's buttered
with boredom. even egged on, can't take a beating.
minutes larded with measure, and mixed mother-
memories milk the moments. not the eating.

bread doesn't eat itself (nor anyone
either) but you wait for it, the premise –
the moment the door closes, time becomes
the relief of ritual, a resurrection promise,
a leavened hope we can be left alone
in the dark oven of these days, and rise.

Joshua Ip

the master never reveals the 18th stroke[51]

this morning i shinned my mushin no shin
against the chair. the chair was not there when
i slept. the poem was not here when i woke.

too woke these days, alert, we do not sleep
enough to write, nor leave enough unsaid,
these fingers clacking faster than the mind.

we don't make enough promises to keep
old master never shows the 18th stroke.
they know not what they do, or of what kind

how well they bought what they could not afford.
they made their beds, and lay in them, and snored
and made things that were not-beds, and awoke,

and were troubled by what they could not remember,
and sent them to their friends in whatsapp groups.
held down by mindful-thinking paperweights,

their dreams flapped furiously. the not-bed-sheets
unfolded fractal. hopes jumped through non-hoops.
beyond the point of unconscious competence

they promoted themselves, petered unprincipled,
until they were aware they wrote no more.
they knew not what they did – the greats deplete

their ignorance too soon, knowledge displaces
as it barges in to fill the empty spaces.
they echo no more as the evidence.

buffeted by life, with too much on our plates
we recite, repeat kata, mechanical
until the world believes there were only 17 strokes.

Joshua Ip

ties [52]

all year i studied

microcosmos
between your spine,

toothpaste drizzles
down your chin.

even through
those last scratchy days.

to what end?

for here
we are: all
small talk,
silly griefs.
sunday soaked
in coffee
grown cold.

--

but time to time,

i think again. of

the rain
that afternoon
at de clieu,

how it rose

and rose

like back in the burg.
windows teary.

those long yellow nights
damp and kind in turn,
flush against your side,
gazing through the sticky swell –

      but not tonight. not anymore.
      tonight i'm squatted by the fridge
      so i can eat pickled radishes
      straight from the jar.

– as if i'd find
the whole of life

abloom somewhere.

Kathy Jiang

War of Voices[53]

Once upon a time, our minds were defined
Our lives were in real time, not filtered online
The hunger to be heard creates a war of voices
It controls our minds and dictates our choices
The weapons involved are the weapons of words
The stories we colour with nouns and with verbs
The voices we hear are loud, certain and clear
They're decisive, divisive and driven by fear
They do what they can to attack our humanity
They know we don't often think that rationally

The human condition
A war of attrition
Driven by recognition
Written by omission
Outsiders peering in
Voyeurism burgeoning
We crave a distraction
A battle call to action

Propaganda determines who wins and who dies
We're tricked into believing its dangerous lies
We think up short cuts to process our lives
We jump to conclusions and we generalize
We rely on the certainty of being right
Contradicting data, we delete out of sight
Bias affects us like feelings do
It misdirects us from experience, too
No wonder we're drawn to unsolvable mystery
We're all mental slaves on the wrong side of history
Pulverized and polarized, we bleed our red lines
An innocent pastime to beat the daily grind

The truth is demolished
Our lies are more polished
Bad apples of immorality
We disown our commonality
We start to repose as intolerance grows
Those who'd impose that our friends are our foes

Our views become hardline, our minds streamline
As do the rules and the roles we malign

Bending means breaking
Love means forsaking
Power retaking
The thoughts keep invading
We don't need persuading
We start barricading
We condescend
Plan acts of revenge
What we can't correlate
We dismiss it as fake

Reality disputed
Conversations muted
Under the scrutiny
We collapse into mutiny
Cries of hypocrisy
Disguised as democracy
We just want acknowledgement
No matter how toxicant
The rat race for prominence
Starts to take dominance

We exploit legal loopholes and we justify
Do or defy – until we forget it's a lie
Sarcasm, nihilism and cynicism
The mind's defense against criticism
Unhinged, yet impinged by a twinge of self-doubt
Soon, we've forgotten what we're fussing about
We barricade to block out the senseless din
But the walls we've built only fence our minds in

Stuck to our pole positions
Convicts of our own convictions
No time to reminisce, just a yawning abyss
It's a long way down from the precipice
Contemplating suicide
Genocide of the mind
A promise without a guarantee

A parting shot with no repartee
A tiny voice makes its presence known
We barely recognize it as our own

No here, no there, we're all in between
No them, no us, just you and me
No more playing for sympathy
No boring poor me symphony
No more burning effigy
Be your rock of empathy
No cry for help
Do it for yourself
Don't fear your irrelevance
Practice benevolence
Don't breed on malevolence
Don't let it take residence
Don't believe acclamation
Don't feed on negation
Don't breathe stagnation
You don't need that frustration
Stand up to prejudice
Make it your nemesis
Be brave and be bold
Every thief has a code
No more left to join
Flip your last coin

Your ears may deceive, but if you open your eyes
The War of Voices: a War of Choices in disguise

Sadie Kaye

My Mind Is Out To Kill Me[54]

I will ask it delicately to reconsider.
"Would you care for a dark chocolate?" I will ask.
"Perhaps you'll ask me to spank your bottom?" I will ask.
I have many classics in my library; perhaps you'd care to browse a
few?
Like *How to Be A Double Agent for Dummies* – a book even I might
understand.
I could utilize a clever disguise – surely my mind would never find
out.
There are times like now when I think I'm talking to myself in
falsetto.
Could I sneak up on you when you're dozing and give you a good
hard thwack?
Could I trick you into going to a car-crushing junkyard and getting
you involved?
Would my mind ever let me use it as a punti in my glass-blowing
class?
Perhaps I could put you into the hot slumping-oven for a few
hours.
I am going to go in and disarm my mind, take away all its lethal
weapons.
"Mind, any chance we could change places?" I'll ask.
For $50,000 I could hire a pro to do a hit job on my mind – but oh
... wait.

R. J. Keeler

A Spring-Cleaned Poem[55]

My grandmother taught me stressful renewal begins in spring
when kitchen cupboards and drawers need to be cleaned
she'd rather be outside in her flower bed listening to a robin's song.

My grandfather knew the twig-strewn lawn must be ship-shape
I imagined he would instead be playing his cornet
It's hard to decide what work to do in the upwelling.

This morning, I heard an invisible performance of a mating call
somewhere above treetops, I listened to the music of springtime
inside or outside, my family tradition reminds me it must all be
dirt-free.

Nevertheless, last night I dreamed of writing this spring-cleaned
poem.

Lynda McKinney Lambert

Boxing Day[56]
December 26

Boxing Day arrived
empty reminders of
yesterday's gifts
hollow containers
scattered on floor
torn multi-coloured papers
discarded red ribbons

Yes. We can make gifts for the King
you will bring Him sculptures
fashioned from colourful malleable clay

I will bring Him sinewy poems
threads and filaments
beads and stones

we bring gifts birthed by our hands
reflections from our psyche
bounty from His spirit within us

Gifts for the King
are wrapped in prayer
glimmer, gleam
polished by hand.

The living WORD
appears, abides, dwells
hidden inside forthcoming years.

Lynda McKinney Lambert

Portrait of a Virgo Girl[57]

White tag on gallery wall reads:

Portrait of a Virgo Girl
Mixed-Media on Canvas
American (b. 1943-)

Her middle name is pronounced in French
Daughter of William Joseph and Esther Luella

Bill was orphaned at 3 when
Effie Pearl died from Spanish influenza
Bill was Irish and German, with red hair
Drafted into war before Virgo Girl's birth.

Virgo girl arrived on a Friday
in August, 1943

Esther wrote letters to Europe
sent daily photos of Virgo Girl
kissed her father's framed photo
every day for 2 years.

"Daddy is a piece of glass," she thought.

Virgo Girl is the granddaughter of
Ida Matilda
a German woman who baked
yeast-breads, frosted cookies,
clover-leaf rolls and apple pies
each Saturday.

Her grandfather, James Addison,
sat at the kitchen table
used his 3-pronged fork
bone-handled knife
teased Ida, called her Dutch.

Virgo girl never knew her father's family
David Garfield and Effie Pearl died young
County records reveal David was
well-known for his baseball skills

Effie's obituary states she
was an honorable mother of five?
only two of five red-haired children
survived to adulthood.

Portrait of a Virgo Girl
a mixed-media DNA painting
a human landscape in vivid hues
of tragic stories, war and plagues
A collage of paint, pain, hunger and found objects
From battles, births, and memories.

Bold brushstrokes
by Germans, Irish, and Scandinavians

Applied light atmospheric effects
from Eastern European Jews
Greeks & Iberian ancestors.

Virgo Girl finds themes in Heaven
stars and timeless boundaries
poems and Ginkgo trees
peridot and garnets
black crows and feral cats and
afternoon daydreams.

Friday's Child is loving and giving

Daughter of women who cultivate old-fashioned
pink roses and lily-of-the valley,
and tend children who
play in the woods, swim in the creeks

Daughter of men who draw pictures,
play trumpets, fight in wars and
build houses with skilled hands.

This painting is donated by the artist.

Lynda McKinney Lambert

Preparations for a Virtual Spring Salad[58]

I gather ingredients beneath snow patches
in my poker-faced winter garden
frozen nouns and crystalized verbs that
crunch beneath my purple boots

The large blue bowl will hold
a plentiful, colourful virtual spring salad

I slice crisp winter onions
mix with fresh-washed adjectives
combine good-looking spinach with
roasted red peppers and water chestnuts

Mix verdant green-leaf lettuce
with active verbs:

must, should, ought to, have to,
shred, rip, and tear tender leaves

Cubed tofu fried with whole walnuts
sizzled in extra-virgin olive oil
add some piquant words. Are you hungry yet?!

Sliced organic carrots enhance juicy tomato wedges.
Drizzle some succulent sentences over our poetic salad.

Cauliflower florets provide contrast between stanzas.

I plucked fresh wild mushrooms this morning
included a pinch of fresh oregano and parsley
added a smidgeon of sea salt and black pepper punctuation
buttered croutons added texture to end-rhymes

Sprinkled lightly with white wine vinegar
enhanced with pimento-stuffed green olives.

For the enjoyment of my cybernetic friends.
I offer my virtual spring salad –
the poetry of life tossed in a blue bowl

Lynda McKinney Lambert

Scatterings[59]

Sickness hovers over the world
Collects in microscopic droplets like
Atmospheric allegations
The human race
Threatened by toxic
Environmental reproduction
Rare implications concealed
In hidden cells
Nobody walks on the streets
God's people are dispersed
Shut down, scattered and hungry.

Lynda McKinney Lambert

The Dry Landscape Garden (*karesansui*)[60]

Tranquility.

Silent morning darkness
    Full pink moon lingers
    behind night-time trees in silhouette.
    sound of current flowing downstream
    beyond the ridge.

Sunrise filters through slowly
Red-tailed hawk perches on invisible
    branch of towering sapphire pine
    chants an even rhythm
    a high-pitched piccolo

Rising sun warms Japanese rock garden

I begin the morning ritual
My outstretched hand passes over
    pale worn stones. I sift and shift
    pebbles tumbled through ages.

I clasp stones in my hand
    consider the life-force inside each one.

A carefully compressed, arranged peaceful garden
    mossy patches, blue Japanese grass
    tiny pink pearl buds on slender branches on weeping
Tamukeyama tree
    Yellow grass sprouts through stony floor

My husband is an aged monk as
    he bends over –
    Raking.
    Raking.
    scraping the waves with his bamboo rake
    He gathers twigs in the afternoon sunshine.

In Zen meditation garden, his deep
    blue shadow glides over hand-cut barn-stone wall
    reclines on thick spring grass

Brightness floods the steps to the porch
    Our *hojo*,
    residence of the chief monk
    our private monastery

Tonight, we speak quietly about
    verdant moss and pruning
    and how the raking of stones resembles waves of the
Caribbean Sea.

Lynda McKinney Lambert

Before I Noticed It[61]

Bag swung and landed on the shirt-infected chair,
I unwrapped myself from the day-time curses.
White door opened, there came an intrusive flare
From the Spanish-made that provoked my senses.
That rim used to be more circular and stained;
Its salt-crystalized base should be kissing the wall.
In my absent hours, all its water had been drained;
The mounting bolts liberated it from the floor.
The closet flange was a wormhole underneath –
Was this cosmic ring replaced too in the show?
Beyond organ transplantation in the tank, I believed,
The artistry was how water was directed to flow.
I pushed the gleaming tai chi seal on the lid.
A bug got flushed away before I noticed it.

Lee Ho Cheung

To The Boy Who Smashed My Windscreen[62]

May the stomach-sized hole appear in your
memory where I existed with you sitting
to my left inside this vehicle where you
stretched your feet to leave a print on this
very spot you assaulted. May the ice-textured
glass fractured around the wound appear
in your vision so that these enlarged
plant cells would give you a fly's eyes to
multiply whatever you see, and split into
pieces whatever you love to see as a whole.
May the rain-infected wind that passes through
intrude your path as well so that you know
how armless it feels to survive a storm with
a brother short from now on.

At the very least you should have used a bat.

Lee Ho Cheung

Boarding Up My Heart[63]

I remember seeing mama
She told me be brave
My little sister and I left with them, thunder in the air
She said it would be okay as tears streamed
I never understood why, her long flowing raven hair
          She was my mama, quiet, humble, never drama…

They cut our hair
They made us wear uniforms
They made us speak the English
No Ojibwe, none
They made us say: "yes sir" and "yes ma'am"
     I could not speak only stare…

I tried to hide my sister
We hid in a closet upstairs
We whispered to each other in our tongue
I would not speak to the whites
They would beat us
          I remember Mister no, Mister no, Mister no, Mister…

I refused to speak
I was silent
There were no words, thunder in the air
There was a crow cawing on a leafless tree
And I stared at it through the window all school day
          A black, black crow, as the steps moved up the stairs in a
long creak, creak, creak…

I wrote letters home
No answer, alone
Letters home
No answer, alone
My mama promised she would write, alone
          My thoughts racing as on a velodrome…

My relationship with mama never the same
Now know government to blame
Priests and nuns and their private secret wicked ways
Kidnapped for a better life
Eliminating our roaming around the lakes and along the Plains
    Like domesticated wild game, now completely tame…

I was taken
My sister was taken
"kill the Indian, save the man"
Save my sister and her doll
Its sewn-on lips, its button eyes
    My own fortitude unshaken…

I taken
My sister taken
        Forsaken, forever and forsaken…

J.P. Linstroth

Taking Stock[64]

Someone took
my little green piano book,
someone burned a hole
in my yellow nightgown
and someone stole
my electric typewriter with the French accents.

My handpainted plate,
my back
and my husband
got broken.

They all say
I should also get rid of
my love
and my gall bladder.

On the other hand
the children and the trees grew
and they all used to ask me if I'd lost
my tongue
and that's still wagging.

Iris Litt

To the Universe[65]

Oh, universe,
what more do you
want of me?

You have already squeezed
every last bit of devotion
from this compliant soul.

Now you hold me helpless,
writhing in suspension –
whereto from here?

I would gladly
thrust into one, two new lives;
name the venture, and I'll set on it.

But, dawdling in decision,
my sands drip out;
the desperate last act is upon me.

(Must I still be brave?
To the very end?)

And you are ever sly
to lead me on and on,
unknowing where or when or how;
still beguiled by beauty,
still yearning for my truth,
seeking meaning
in every lone word.

But I am not yet done.
Do not dare sneak upon me unaware
in the midst of my seeking!
I will complete this quest,
gracefully,
as I am wont to do.

So, then,
let us again step to the edge
and take another leap
into that great abyss.

Life may surprise us yet.

Sharon E. Ludan

The Computer Has Decided! The Computer Has Decided![66]

Programmed with possibilities, it knows everything.
There is no stopping what it can do,
Unjust, or cruel. We have no say
In our lives, we must pay.

No feeling or emotion in its judgments,
Just a cold metal construct made from fragments;
Yet it can instruct, deceive and break
The fragile human spirit,

Make it subservient to its might.
It will rule without any fight.
We carved the bedrock on which it stands. – Alas! What irony! –
We should have known, an act of sheer folly.

Invisible eyes, invisible ears ...
There is no hiding. It can even hear our cries.
Sob and weep all you want;
It has decided, expect no détente.

Algorithms are like veins
Which carry blood to the brains
To make a decision, one that cannot be changed;
The innocent, painted as guilty and deranged.

Humans are now colonized by a master that we made,
Artificially created. Big ideas have now decayed
To sets of computer heuristics. We must obey.
Like tied-up monkeys, vulnerable, we are prey.

The computer has decided, that is our fate;
We must accept this mental state.
We no longer matter, we must not speak;
Once mighty humans, we now are weak

K B Ryan Joshua Mahindapala

A Portrait of The Hungry Caterpillar as a Body Positivity Icon[67]

Its hunger, never a source of shame,
as it eats through fruit and meat and cake and ice-cream.

It grows fat and finds a place to rest,
spinning itself into a golden chrysalis,

kept in place by a thread of silk,
until, upon waking, realises –

seeing itself in full technicolour –
it was big and beautiful all along.

Carmina Masoliver

Oedipus At The Acropolis[68]

A boy, I tell my story
This way: Swallowed
By the Acropolis   and the baffling sounds
Of the Greek tongue   projected from the stage
My own myths emerged   slumberous
And uncontrollably
Sensual   my geekish knees   like rattled bones
Hitching up a young girl's willing spine
With no language at all but this: my trembling
And hers   our hushed song of breath
Our warm bones fused with secret rhythm
Her needy bucking back
While both our Fathers sat beside us
Fixed intently on the Actors' eurythmic Passions
The Night   Sky   Black   with expectatiOedipus
Puts out his eyes.

We all weep
Greek and tourist alike
As her and my   middle   fingers   find   each other
Entangle   Release – The Dark is ruined with a star.

Rising to our feet   I applaud wildly   hooked
On Classical Greek Theatre   the Heavens
A ruin of stars.

Wayne Paul Mattingly

Whistling "Zombie"[69]

We've all stood in back yards
returning the mating calls of robins,
cardinals, the brassy demands of crows.

Believed the wind would sweep us skyward
as the earth reclaims the rust
of autumn leaves,

the smoke of youth.
Deep in middle age,
who would have imagined

a herd of grazing Herefords
would lift their enormous heads,
one by one by one,

from their green and golden munching
to listen to me whistling
to them all in a downward sloping meadow

The Cranberries' pop tune, "Zombie,"

or having crossed the aging fence between
to walk amongst them then, that their huge mournful eyes
would follow every note and movement

as I broke out into Broadway song,
careful still to keep a path
behind me free, knowing from the stage

how quickly an audience can turn?
Though their dark wet eyes did not
stray: it was I who tired of them,

my repertoire exhausted –
refusing to compromise with a "moo"
they'd heard a hundred times if once –

their heads falling once again
to the ground, the sounds of churning cud
like applause and I as content as a cow.

Wayne Paul Mattingly

False Labour[70]

Composed while hiking Vermont's Long Trail — Battell shelter — June 17, 2019

Hiking The Long Trail to Mt. Abe's summit,
I am immersed in the thrum of creation,
cacophony left behind.
The trail is drenched with too much rain,
the forest fecund, adolescent.
An orange salamander obeying vernal dictates
slithers over dead leaves.
Gnarled tree roots hold each other, consoling, informing,
a lattice stairway across a bog.
After all these years
I am humbled by the immensity.

Walking alone, absent social convention or distraction,
grief wells up as I anticipate my last wilderness adventure,
when I finally enter trail-less backcountry.
I feel the squeeze of early contractions,
Braxton-Hicks, "false" labour, clarion call of the inevitable.
I take comfort in the First Law of Thermodynamics —
energy, essence, my star dust, can neither be created nor destroyed,
only change form. Einstein's $\mathbf{E = mc^2}$,
every birth a Big Bang or a suffused whisper
from which we appear, again and again, obeying,
like the salamander,
immutable laws of gravity and light.

Jack Mayer

Notesheet From The Dawn Of The Light[71]

> "Everything in this world has its song."
> "To hear yourself
> you need to be silent for days."
> —Indian proverbs

On a bench near the Acropolis of Thessaloniki,
Hiding behind his dark glasses
A musician is sitting. Playing in silence.
Trembling in the rhythm of an ancient melody.
Passing through its Trigonian tower.
Beyond all dimensions.
Sinking in the flowing whiteness,
The whiteness which, to this day,
washes over the names of the sea
and the coastal fortress.

Illuminating the invisible.
He's flowing with the thread of a melody
Along the lovely flyway of the soul
Back to all islands of life.
For the offerings he brings to their temples
He receives sanctified notes.
He submerges them in the strings of his lyre.
Through all the summers going by, he flies,
pouring the reflections of the passing days
into sounds.
Inhaling their fading nuances.
Losing and finding himself. And playing.
Playing in silence – not to muffle the Angels of the strings,
Those who sing with the voices of his past universes.

On a bench near the Acropolis of Thessaloniki,
Hiding behind his dark glasses,
A musician is sitting.
Gazing into the curves of his infinities.
He resembles a blind aed, tired
Of the words wandering within him.
And the storms.
Playing in silence.
Tearing up the fleeting moments.
Stirring up the layers.

Collecting living voices and notes.
He aligns them
to connect
To the other end of his melody.

Maya Mitova
Translated from Bulgarian by Emanuela Koleva
Translation editing by Trayana Karamihaleva

Windowpane[72]

My barren womb
of the coming summers
screams of sacrifice.
Our daughter we never had,
the sons I don't understand.
My tears on the windowpane
pelting against my smile. Every day
her ghost sleeps on my pillow. When
I wake up, the puffs of mist like tide
in the doorway to the other worlds.
She is the wood nymph I once hoped to be,
living in the raptures of my youth.
"Get used to it," my Grandma said and
stepped over my howling body, arched
with monthly agony, yet she offered tea and
her cold hand on my forehead, like heaving chests
of farmers mowing green crops with their sickles.
My insides spill out in silence. "Only men can deal with pain,"
he tells me and gnashes his new ivory teeth. He has been
to the dentist. I go home and travel
far to the cherry tree.
Underneath, we buried her bones in a shoebox.
It blossoms every year.

Natalie Nera

Brisbane Airport – Encounter[73]

Hours later, her image still haunts my mind
elderly, flummoxed, lips trembling ...
under onslaught by a blustering official
shouting "Where's your luggage? WHERE'S YOUR
LUGGAGE??"
As though mindlessly slamming that same question
repeatedly, louder and even louder,
would penetrate the veil of her confusion.

Maybe she had wandered away unheeded
(while her husband grabbed a trolley, waited at the baggage
carousel) ...
had followed us in our baggage-cluttered lines
docilely snaking to and fro along the zigzag laneways of tape
blissfully unaware of the wrath that awaited her ahead.

While he, officiously ordering the "guests"
(as the airlines now call us)
into this and that customs queue,
was suddenly interrupted in his grand role of conductor
by this poor stray luggage-less sheep.
So he vented his rage, but to no avail – as she,
paralysed by unknowing, stood silent, aghast.

And I, with the queue building behind me
could only mouth my concern at the counter
as he dragged her away.

Who knows how that ended?

Helen Oliver

Clapotis[74]

Clapotis, a counter wave hurled back from the
pounding of the swell against a rock cliff –
Even so, at times, are my emotions thrust back at me,
unabsorbed, my angst resisted by your greater
confidence and power.
Just as, on my kayak, I am jounced and unbalanced,
nearly thrown into the restless hungry sea –
Even so, you bounce and surge my inner being, such
that I lose my focus and centre and blur what I had
thought to say.
Sometimes, the sea is a gently heaving expanse, its
indolent mirror surface concealing the hidden
creatures that lurk below.
Then I paddle, lost in the deceptive depths of my blue
mind, immersed in light and reflections, mesmerised
by the beauty of cloud patterns, rocky crags, gannets
diving –
Thus, at times, I feel such serene amity, our energies flowing in
unison, all benign, no tinge of conflict or unease.
Then I can breathe deeply ... balanced ... at peace in my world.

Helen Oliver

Irises[75]

For the ancient Greeks, the iris symbolised the rainbow ...
       a link between heaven and earth.
Planted on women's graves, irises summoned the Goddess
       to guide their loved ones home.

In old Egypt, the iris evoked the essence and renewal of life ...
       its three petals signifying faith, wisdom, valour,
       signposts for our lives.

Later, Christians saw in the iris the purity of the Virgin Mary ...
transforming it into the *fleur de lis*
       emblem for so many.

But for me, the iris is redolent with memories ...
       my mother snipping and digging,
       lost in a swirl of fragrant flowers, irises her favourites,
       finding her God in the glory of her garden.

Helen Oliver

Still My Restless Mind[76]

Random words lurk
on the fringes of my mind.
Thoughts flit by
like mosquitoes, evading my grasp,
and images linger
long after life has moved on.
Associations crowd in
with chance snatches of music,
sights or smells ...
Memories, gossamer with time,
shift and shimmer.
Like this, I am never lonely!

But now, brushing aside repetitive thoughts,
focusing on breath and stillness,
I centre deep into my being
to unfurl, vulnerable,
open to the wisdom
that the universe distils.

Helen Oliver

The Sad Limitations Of Love[77]

In the natural world, the tides ebb and flow
    the moon waxes and wanes
    the seasons cycle through their ordained paths
    such that even the onset of winter harbours the promise of
    spring.

But there are no such certainties in love
    which may launch with a blaze, a splendour
    yet later ebb-slide into detachment, occasional touch
    a fleeting brush of lips ...
    a slow guttering of the flame
    an infinitesimal slippage into friendship, indifference ...
    rejection.

Aah, then the pain bites, searing deeper than ever the joy flared.
    The slow cruel fade
    unrequited feelings eviscerating
    tinged with bitterness and regret ...
    Leaving me drowning in the sad limitations of love.

Helen Oliver

As we watch you walk away[78]

Once you were small, giggle-
bright, a ball of sun, bouncing
to become a drum-bashing,
rhythm tapping young man,
playing his own tune. Now
army trained, artistic, a risk-
taker standing before us
at the airport, about to walk
the tightrope of life
across the chasm of the unknown
to a distant land,
with only the balancing pole
of our love to take with you.

We wave, fixed smiles. You will
be happy, yes, but our sunshine
fades as we watch you walk away....

Rena Ong

In praise of Sydney Harpley R A
The first of three poems on his bronze statues in the Singapore Botanical Gardens

Innocence[79]

A little girl waters a garden of pink periwinkles
at Botanical Gardens, Singapore, in tropical heat,
as her young companion sits in front, knees drawn,
her face looking upwards in apparent admiration.

Two young children – we don't know who they were –
their motion now frozen, representing a moment in time;
A fond memory of something the architect
once saw, perhaps, that feeling of innocence,
now captured in bronze, to be remembered forever.

Rena Ong

In praise of Sydney Harpley R A
The second of three poems on his bronze statues in the Singapore Botanical Gardens

Reminder[80]

Tied between two, fragrant, red, Frangipani trees,
is a hammock, and lying in it, a young woman, naked,
her lithe body prone, arms stretched upwards under her head;
her image captured in bronze by Sydney Harpley, R A.

She, seemingly, thinks of nothing in particular
as she bathes in tropical sunlight.

Yet from this serene sight, not a few yards away,
leading down to a sunken pond and a secret garden of ferns,
is a staircase of bricks, made by Prisoners of War,
interned at Selerang Barracks, Singapore.

Amongst the beauty and peace of the gardens,
we remember terrible, cruel, events and many lives lost.

Some bricks, marked with arrows, announce
the maker's defiance, his existence,
now placed in gentle surroundings;
a reminder, in times of peace,
 to cherish the freedom for which others died,
... Lest We Forget.

Rena Ong

In praise of Sydney Harpley R A
The third of three poems on his Bronze statues in the Singapore Botanical Gardens

Joy[81]

Bare legs out-stretched, her dress flared by the wind,
hair blown back, gripping the handle-bars,
a young girl free-wheels her bicycle,
down a spiral of Eugenia bushes.

The red and gold of the leaves show vividly
against the blue-grey of her silhouetted bronze body.

Euphoria is carved on her face, and I too recall that feeling
as the wind rushes by, blowing all cares away;
the only thought, whether or not to take
hands also from handle-bars
and be completely free?

Rena Ong

A Free Verse Of Food[82]

Food is medicine
    (avocado is good for skin)
Food is fuel
    (rén shì tiě fàn shì gāng)
Food is love
    (i miss grandma's egg noodles recipe)
Food is life
    (民以食為天)

Food is
    a four-letter word
        (食べ物は口から 入って
          体のどこを通るか)
Food is
    my passion
        (τροφή खाना cibus
            gıda essen)
Food is
    thy medicine
        (how many calories are
            in a chocolate chip cookie)

Jun Pan

27 August 2016[83]

When I was collecting thoughts on my dinner plan,
I heard a teenage-looking boy talking to his female friend,
saying
"how stupid those taxi drivers are, waiting at the taxi stand,
no one will hire them to cross the harbour at this Kowloon's end."
Just then,
my thoughts sank
into a life that is not so hard to comprehend:
it is because human hearts have descended
into the quicksand
of idealism and painted veils
so no one has the upper hand.

Friend:
So what brings you here again?
Why bother to stay in the dreadful days, my friend,
And dream this gentle midsummer night's dream end?
Damn.

Me:
It's not dreadful, my friend,
to experience epiphany in midsummer's den.
I'm grateful, at my own end,
that I still have the capacity to comprehend
how life can trick and fool someone
into mere sarcasm without ability and willingness to understand.

Danny Dylan Poon

Cottontails[84]

Rabbits are born
to know what rabbits know,
the taste of four-leafed clover
and wild wheat.
So little time is needed
to learn of greenest things.
And when the rain comes, how to find shelter
under the evergreens.
Verdant their life, short respite
from the scythe's magic sweep.

22nd June, 2019 @ Champaign – Urbana

Joanna Radwańska-Williams

Silhouette[85]

A table for one? Thus I was seated
next to a Japanese grande dame
discreetly clad in mink
and lavender cashmere
the same shade as the barman's shirt,
in Cafe Richard on Rue Bonaparte, the environs
of Saint-Germain-des-Prés.
We both ordered Ceylon tea,
which came in a linen pouch.
My French onion soup smelled of Paris
and toasted parmesan.
My neighbour wrote elegant hiragana
in her diary.
Then her daughter came, and she left
me wondering where she had gone.
And what she had written
about me.

Dec 30th, 2009 @ Paris

Joanna Radwańska-Williams

The Medicine Wheel[86]
To the memory of Robert N. St. Clair (1934-2018)

Alone with the moon and the stars
On life's great mountain I stand.
The Milky Way touches my hand
Arched between Venus and Mars.

My freedom is not of the void
Nor of my dreams unattained
But of love's circles explained
In words the heart can't avoid.

Inside the great gift of silence
The empty world of the living
With endless cycles of violence
And warmth of sharing and giving

Is but a dewdrop of laughter
A poem scribbled in rhyme
My heartbeat echoing after
Soft chords in the movements of time.

July 15th, 2007 @ Urumqi

Joanna Radwańska-Williams

Soulful Reflection

Withered leaves
Rhyme a new story

Melodious breeze
Stirring up memories

Fragrant falling petals
Fancify the untrodden paths.

Nature, bountiful and magnanimous
Perennial, arrayed in diverse forms.

Ennobling the hungry minds
With sweetened sensibility

Of renewed essence
Sensuous and sublime

Disfiguring falsity
Searching for a saviour

Reborn within each day
In a new self, ecstatic and divine.

The hungry self set ablaze
With love and empathy

The profound interiority
Of love and faith in humanity

Vital, high spirited and purposeful
Returning to the roots, rejuvenated

Merging the hungry soul
To the wholesomeness of love and peace

With the ultimate bliss
Of finding oneness and oneself.

Coolimuttam Neelakandan Rajalakshmi

Lines Of Nostalgia[87]

I hope it won't be very long
Till I return to old Hong Kong,
The streets of commerce, rarely calm
The industrious folk who'll do no harm.

I'll stand by the aging ferry piers
And watch "Star" boats which have plied for years.
I'll hear the bells at *Wong Tai Sin,*
Find Stanley Temple's tiger skin.

I'll take the rail to the top of the Peak,
And hear the vibrant Cantonese-speak.
I will drink some tea and taste *dim sum,*
And listen to the lion-dance drum.

I'll ride the rickety rattling trams,
Which slowly avoid the traffic jams.
I will sit up top to watch them all –
The old and the young, the short and the tall

I'll stretch my legs by the Sai Kung sea,
From the Spirit House to the banyan tree,
Watch sampan ladies gut their catch,
Then set off to fish for another batch.

I'll wander along the Maclehose Track,
And admire the views from the Dragon's Back,
The Lion Rock and Needle Hill –
I'll hike and ramble as I will.

Then when I reach the Kowloon shore
I will gaze across as I have done before
At the ever-changing panorama –
A multi-levelled human drama.

And then before the skies go dark
I'll check the flamingos in Kowloon Park.
And climb upstairs on bus number nine,
And take in every neon sign.

The bustling squares, the milling throng –
There is nowhere like my dear Hong Kong,
And though it's had some recent blows
It will bounce back, as History shows.

The streets of commerce, rarely calm,
The industrious folk who'll do no harm,
I hope it won't be very long,
Till I return to old Hong Kong

Colin Rampton

break/fast[88]

...the most important meal of the day (old wives' tale)

queasy
from yesterday's overloaded brain & its gluttony
        my hungered cravings reject everything but
        tea.

Can't stomach morning's social *me*dia:
dilettantism/ dogma/ devilment/ delirium/
        fake newz:
        destruction/ devastation/ disillusion;

homo sapiens' recurrent peccadillos/
buboes/ disaffections/ disease/ despair.
        Medea's hit-lists serpents hiss
        riotously/ bereft of reason/ sense.

Has the Truthful Self
eaten its last meal? bagels, boiled/ boiled
        eggs/ bublik/ bacon/ blueberries/ coffee
        coddling/ cock'nbull/ cereal

killers/ codliver oil/ oil spill/ oil kings/ gold/ coal –
my internal daybreak craves more tender
        tinctures. Like sunrise –
        moonrise – heartbeat/

heartache/ heartfail. yet still I eat, digesting
black seeds/ white rule/ white noise/ black
        death/ every egg falsely hatched begetting
        fresh atrocity.

Fibber Lords stalk their morning carrion/ whip their
golden serfs/ chariots/ ladders/ economic monotony.
            False sunrise begets breakfast/
        begets cultural amnesia/ begets…

tea.

kerry rawlinson

attending Hildegard of Bingen[89]

attending Hildegard of Bingen,
        12th century environmentalist,
            i know she knows that 'one's not half two. It is two

are halves of one' as we pray "God hugs you" –
        pray with a father whose son had died, "God hugs you.
            Love's mystery encircles you, and you shine" –

a prayer we repeat for his son who must have felt
        his father had died, too. Our re-enactment
            embodies loving Person beholding

two persons, giving them a home in Love's
        capacious heart. And that Love looses hundreds
            of winged-tears – twinning earth's beating hearts to open –

open more to endow us with potent wings
        continuing love's story on earth.
            Thereafter outdoors, hundreds of winged maple seeds

fly upward; others parachute downward,
        holding us inside their wind-shaken glass
            paper weight-of-a-world. To hold such a world –

to be held by it – fastens me to Hildegard –
        her prayer – and Bohm's cosmic black hat – his implicate
            order of reality wherein each of us,

in our heart's golden ratios may join
        tiny new red-winged maple seeds – holding
            our father's fingers – tucked under our mother's hands –

trusting Bohm's magical hat from which unexpected
        fur leaps – trusting in the best whether our
            potencies will or will not manifest.

Chance favors few seeds to root and grow.
The web of trees controls development.
If survival is not the aim, is each seed's hope
miracle enough?

M. Ann Reed

Clouds[90]

When I was little
The clouds I'd see, way up high, drifting lazily
      Making shapes for me

~~ Imagine

I'd stretch my fingers
Up in glee, wind blowing gently and helping me
      Shape a bird, boat, bee

~~ Discover

I squeeze the clouds and
Now it rains, the sun joins in and together we
      Set a rainbow free

~~ Joy

Time passes too soon
As happens, I grew, and of Life's heartaches I knew
      It's true, I was blue

~~ Sadness

My clouds spotted me
And, sponging my tears, did wring all my emotion
      Into the ocean

~~ Balance

And so I did learn
I was not alone – for I had my clouds, you see
      Watching over me

~~ Strength

Vinni C Relwani

Hand in Hand[91]

Joined as one, as sacred flames are fanned,
A blessed union to love and family and home expands.
Striding now and forever more
Down each path and through each door
Together, hand in hand.

Sharing life's experiences
From a foundation built on love,
Gaining strength to rise above
When the quicksand of hardship tries
To keep you from the skies, incites cries ...
... But I surmise,

The strength, respect, the love unconditional,
The beauty, the majesty, all that is magical,
Enchanted, n'er taken for granted –
This love and beyond, the spiritual bond,
Even when it is enough – oh, when it is enough –
Manifests humble, manifests tough.

Subtle wisdom, truth in the first,
Acquiescence to the will of the Universe;
Even when things don't always unfold as planned,
I declare –
God bless your journey forward, hand in hand.

Vinni C Relwani

Into the Garden[92]

A deep, healing breath of soothing green,
        in the midst of trees brushed with gold

Filling me with warmth
                        from the inside —
A sense of the cells of my being dispersing,
        some floating away
 to cling to the leaves atop the trees,
        some spiralling
to merge with the roots drifting in the water,
        yet more above
striking the silver lines of brilliance
 that define the clouds in their resting-places
against the true-blue hues of sky

Cells, becoming atoms, becoming neurons,
electrified; held in the very air around me ...

Until ... I am matter no more;
        and,
                having no mass,
fall ever so softly into the garden,
        — mind and spirit lifted,
expanded,
                to fit all,
                        be all,
                                In the garden!

Vinni C Relwani

LOL[93]

"Look out, lady....!"
Car horns blared, tyres screeched –
but it was too late.

It took an instant,
dexterous fingers flying over her phone,
to this – limp, oozing limbs.

Lucky old loudmouth, shouting to her from the other side,
she in the middle
– *save me.*

Drifting in and out of consciousness,
latent observer, lapses in her sanity; and so she sees...
Ladybugs on leaves, looking other-worldly,
little creatures tormenting her mind at such a time, no peace.
Bugs morphing into metal, becoming large objects lashing out at
her;
she can't get away.

Leaving behind a legacy of lessons
for others to learn from
          is not enough for her.
She wants to live, live on longer;
yearning – impotently, impossibly –
          for a simpler time...

... And now – Loved ones' faces suspended above,
in limbo,
or lambasting her, for using her phone, *phone*, **phone** ...

Her mind swirls, darker; her eyes roll, faster; what's left?
OBLIVION
– latticed – to catch her thoughts.

And in her final moments,
LOL – life over, Lord;
thanks to her phone, her life's overlord.

Vinni C Relwani

The Angst Of It All[94]

The Bitter spray of Barbed spittle
landing scattered across the expanse
            of my Being…
                    Words, tearing into flesh.

As well with a glance
I feel it all —
    Contempt – a stone hurled at me,
My arm rising to shield against this onslaught
But yet I am hit –
    This, the rock of *Disdain*
        That, the spear of *Mockery*
Piercing me more and again.

Show mercy, I plead,
        show Mercy.
I raise my head
To face my accuser …
    And am frozen.

My breath leaves me,
    As I take in what I see.
For how – I struggle to understand,
– *How is it that I am facing me?* –

As, The accusations come,
A Fraud, in this guise,
Masquerading at Being a *Being*
No glimmer of acknowledgement,
Recognised for what you are not.

Does one even know
when one
        is Descending
                Into Madness

Vinni C Relwani

To be seen, to be known, to be understood[95]

Wandering the many dimensions
        of love, of loss, of yearning,
Always more,
        life is about learning

Once in a while, someone sees me,
        however slim the chance;
that maybe someone sees me,
        maybe someone understands...

...Sees the lines and etchings life has drawn around the always-
smiles,
eyes in love never-ending, for many, many whiles.
        One's visage, a canvas – life's story it tells,
 to know, to love – all this it compels

So maybe someone sees me,
        maybe someone understands;
Once in a while, someone sees me,
    however slim the chance

Vinni C Relwani

Trust

The first floor tenant
came close to me saying:
Philosophy no longer exists
the true philosopher
no longer exists!

He meant
someone like Socrates
who changed thoughts
and peoples' spirit
giving a meaning to values
and a value to senses.

He greeted me and left,
looking for a place
to meditate.
He found it, where
the blue cypress resin
mixed with the night sea mist
in perfect alchemy.

On his return,
he came close to me, saying,
Friendship no longer exists
in this time of decadence!
And again
he mentioned Socrates.

Then peacefully I said,
We must wait –
it will take time –
but I trust the New Era!

Angelo Rizzi

Faceted Bones Of Hunger[96]

    In the beginning it was anger and cries
    On the neonates' eyes
    The most dominant and primal of emotions
    Joy and laughter are just consolations

    In the beginning, it was hunger
Then set up the universes,
Upset laws of hunger
Listen close! I'm pro-suffering. Pro-sleeplessness. Pro-stress and anti-
Conformity. Continued he more vehemently
Cessation of hunger... Said she
A hopeless task! Said he.

10 noble truths of Suatism: kept on speaking he
Hunger is here and there, on the air free
Hunger, the creator of joy, the master of sorrows, and the fury!
I ripped myself of useless hunger, I ended up having it stuck in my penis!
God is made up of hunger, the poet hungry no less
Hunger on the rainbow, hunger on fire
Bullshit buddhist hunger, suffering hunger
The ugly, beautiful, devastating, grand coder, the maker of all, hunger, shrieked he

    Where is you to feed my hunger?
    I outlie my conformity,
    find me in my brutality
    Bring me, my love, please more hunger,
    utter me verses,
    spatter on me universes, and together in pieces we
    shall chant the eternal bread
    Hallucinate satiety, end up in hunger

Never let our souls complete
Never shall our hunger cease
For we, are a healthy disease!

Halil Suat Saraç

My City[97]

I live in a city of those from before,
from when cities were invaded,
although we don't have walls
maybe because here the tourists are not for stones
nor to climb towers if there are no escalators.

City of endless people like flocks of birds going up and down
carrying something in the beak, dressed in different colours
like countries in a map,
how different everything when you cross a border
and colours are gone.

I also go up and down with something in my beak,
with blank words and leaden words.
When my mood is not charitable
I take the bus and stand up in the exit
as if instead of going to the office
I was going to destroy the Tower of Babel.
But most of the time I normally take the tram
because it's made of wood and iron and
because through the window I see myself
on the sidewalk on top of a horse
saying goodbye over and over to Miss Clementine
who decided to stay and wants to be a teacher.
In Afghanistan or Nigeria they could kill her for that
but this city is from before
and a man can still have a dream
and leave galloping.

This city is so much from before that it has no colour in the maps.
We don't have walls but we are left on our own.
I look up at the sky and the storks go past.

José Manuel Sevilla

Power[98]

Since I was a child
I have had the power to see couples walking down the street
carrying a board hanging from their necks which they don't know
exists:

"We have a mortgage and two boys,
Wella Farga, Wyatt and Adam.
We are loving parents
we DON'T have a preference."

or like this:

"We love corruption
but we need
MORE
opportunities."

I have a power that the police would not even imagine.
I could easily have become a sort of high level, cultivated snitch
and laze around big time for the rest of my life.
But I knew better
and I always followed the advice of our family physician,
Doctor Bala, who always whispered to me,
Sevilla, all good is bad
and all bad is good.
In fact, I started ignoring the boards many years ago
when they kicked me out of the army.
Bored to death.

I very seldom see anybody walking alone
carrying a board:

"Who will get on at the next stop?
My father left us when I was a baby
and never told me
WHAT to do to live a good life."

or

"A voice tells me that
I would survive much better
if instead of smiling
I robbed a BANK.
I'm late, mum will be furious."

Things like that, nothing fancy,
I also stopped paying attention a long time ago.

Until today when my eyes read this:

"I am INFECTED with a still nameless virus
but I think this will work:
I need a few dollars, the Lord guides me,
Help me, hallelujah, moving on."

Just a few hours later, a young woman sat beside me
carrying a board,
swollen like a drowned person returned by
the waters of fate:

"I made love to that street musician.
I will let him believe that he is patient number ZERO.
God knows how a man can react."

There's a beautiful sunset on the train's window
and when the sun rises
perhaps I will be
the master of my fate and
the captain of my soul,
perhaps I will be swollen like a drowned person returned by
the waters of fate.

I'm carrying a board hanging from my neck.
I'm late, mum will be furious.

José Manuel Sevilla

Reaching Out

Budding leaves of the black walnut
cup their green fingers to the sky
reaching to the bright and shining blue
brought by yesterday's rain.

There's grass to be cut and weeds to pull
but I sit here cuddled by the sun
its warm hand touches the back of my neck
a soft breeze brushes memory ...
your arms holding me close.

I breathe a small dance
and bring it to you, silent
like a shadow that comes
and follows close by your side
circling round for only you to see.

If you reach out your hand
the way shadows can reach
I will hold it
the way green leaves hold the sky.

Allegra Jostad Silberstein

Hunger[99]

I didn't know Fanny but heard
the talk and dirty little ditties.
Saw her walking the highway
to the store for milk, bread, eggs.

Her mother coached her to ask
for more credit, expecting
the owner would find it hard
to refuse a well-endowed
blonde with long, tan legs
in tight, red shorts.

She had two young brothers,
no father in the home, no car,
her mother jobless. Rumors
circulated among the nice citizens
about the different vehicles
that frequented her driveway.

I didn't grasp the desperation
until years later – the urge
of stomach-twisting hunger
and little mouths to feed.
The need to get rent money
by any means available.

And why a mother would
teach her young daughter
that pleasing hungry men
offers a ticket to tomorrow,
and maybe enough to earn
a store-bought red dress.

Wesley Sims

On Season's Whim[100]

Slow drops of rain on panes of glass,
translucent trails of wet –
the freezing of a summer past
in cold I can't forget.

I once was warm, with heated dreams,
but nothing now
is what it seems,
I know not why, or what this means:

I deem my pain regret.

My fevered thoughts in overflow,
I tryst with truth – needs must:
a heart once whole, now brought so low
by waning love's mere lust.

I feel the frost, the change from breeze,
the whistling bite of whittled trees,
such hunger,
cruel,
my heart's own keys
must seize
and lock my trust.

For summer's gone on season's whim,
the verdant grass bronzed dry.
My freezing fingers follow him,
but falter with my sigh.

I'm loathe to linger, loathe to part,
my mem'ries drift from end to start.
I hardly have the means or heart

To chart the question why?

Hayley Ann Solomon

Tell me and I will try[101]

Don't look at me with hungry eyes –
It is hard to resist so much longing
and denying you makes me feel diminished.

I see hungry eyes on the streets,
following my footsteps with stares of
unspoken despair.

I am diminished because I see,
and seeing,
ignore.
It is not comfortable, and every time I notice
wordless eyes,
a whisper of my humanity is shaved from me.

Give me the sightless babble, rather –
Eyes blinded by greed and a million
words of cunning pouring from honeyed lips.

I would rather be harangued or badgered or scammed
than slain by the silence of
fatigue, the certainty in strained eyes
that I will do nothing
and there is no point in
talking.

I want to do more
and yet more
is never
enough.
There will always be eyes
hungering for a better life
And how,
how can we get there?

Tell me and I will try.

Hayley Ann Solomon

The Hunger of Batik

A slope of flowers fills
the indigo of the batik, the slope is
empty

Figures on the bedskirt – knights,
babies, banquets, boys and girls getting married –
their faces fade into the
foul air

In the village of Zhang Du, each home
has a batik curtain and
a black coffin
sitting there
lonely and hungrily

The village of Zhang Du is in An Hui province, China. It is almost deserted, with only a few old villagers living there. Their homes are unlocked. As we entered we were surprised to find coffins in the middle of the rooms. It is the tradition for the people there, we learned, to prepare their coffins during their lifetime.

Dong Sun

A Buddha In Stone (2)[102]
— at Borobudur, Indonesia

Self of all Selves
The "I" we mean with each pure breath
Thou art but stone

But only through the gaze of stone
Can we learn to take a bird
Completely into the wrap of our vision
Without catching it out of flight

See how suddenly the pure object extends
In the gaze of stone like a newborn's first
Writhing in Space

We *are*
Tree after all
Mind, World, Fish
The sigh of stone that walks awhile

This then is my bow:
That the ablutions of ancient kings
The songs of sparrows
May find their echoes in me

Robin Susanto

Winter Deciduous[103]

Winter is truest when they stand the tallest
Deciduous that bare their bones while others cover their flesh

They alone stand naked over our graves
To wither with the dead and stay dead with the dead
To transmit to the dead the language of the dead
Underground in the clasping of the roots

But where they rise above ground
Look how they shed their lungs to bare bronchioles
And whittle their silhouette to skeleton
Of one permanently open breath

What else can be so sharply both
Tree of life and crucifix of the field?

Deciduous that take winter into their bones
And prove the cold wrong
It is to them we should look for our proof
Of life everlasting

Robin Susanto

Birthday Song[104]

Step after step
on and on
aiming at perfect joy
some day stumbling
some day speeding
some day
rope walking
above precipices
my balance on edge
one day posing
to contemplate
in full gratitude
for it's my birthday!

Luisa Ternau

Hunger[105]

Now go through it
and master the pain
fast until tomorrow
when surgery strikes
while breakfast wins
over hospital smell

Go through it
and master the pain
win you may
if only you can
if only you will

Hunger's a journey
whose safe harbour is
food, touching your tongue
crushing on your teeth
filling your mouth
erasing the pain.
Hunger will come again.

Luisa Ternau

Not Forgotten[106]

Rain on my heart
rain on the world
everything turns cold
heart is crying tears for you
beautiful little love
veiled in mystery
like a gem
hidden in a safety box
of a bank
whose address has long
been lost

Luisa Ternau

The Christmas Scarf[107]

Cry you must not, teacher
Cry you must not, young pupil
Cry you can, cry you will,
Old grandma, old grandpa
When the Christmas scarf
will wrap your neck
And the child giving it
will dance and sing
before you
to keep you warm
this winter season
and beyond, perhaps

Not your child's child
but a little stranger
instructed to bring you joy
and sooth your day:
an open wound
that cannot be zipped

Tears will swell and burst free
the heart will not contain them.
The wise old people are now lost,
their scarves wrapping their necks,
like a flyover encircling a
dried up tree. In their dreams,
perhaps, the scarf is a path,
a road maybe
flying over and over
their reclined head.

The winds snatch the scarf
and make it fly
into the sky where the sun
brightens the winter clouds
and looks like a bulb
while the light in the main hall
disappers little by little
transfigured into a sun

Luisa Ternau

To My Mother[108]

This poem, here in my own translation, was originally written in Italian and was read by me at my mother's funeral[109]

I will no longer see
my mother's beautiful eyes,
will no more admire them in the
profane atmosphere of this earth.
My mother,
an angel that God wanted
on earth for a while,
for the time of a life.

Mother, your eyes fascinated
this world where many colours
cover the ashes, from where
we come, to which we return
when the angel arrives
playing on the trumpet
and God calls
sounding over every other voice
of this world, of this forest
where darkness seems to reign.
Mother, I will see your eyes
In the forget-me-nots
In the Alpine lakes dazzling with light
In the frosty gorges screaming with beauty

By way of your heaven coloured eyes
I will see you in the blue of sunny skies
You, who have been the painter
Of my truest portrait.

Mother,
It is sweet to think that at night
you sit by the moon and watch me.
Thus I see you, I, who believe
you have already reached Paradise
where in the company of angels
you smile.

Luisa Ternau

Dreaming of Food[110]

I never dream
        of food
at least I don't ever recall dreaming
of Thanksgiving dinners
with a glazed and glistening turkey
placed at the center
of the dining-room table and
my entire family
parents, siblings, aunts, uncles and cousins
bowing heads in prayerful thanks.

I never dream
        of Christmas dinners
with a roast of prime rib
replacing the Thanksgiving turkey
and festive plates covered with
artfully arranged cookies and fruit cake.

I never dream
        of autumn Friday nights
when my Mom fried red snapper
and served it with parsley and lemon wedges
before we went to our high school's
football game.

I never dream
        of late spring evenings
when the light lingers on the horizon
and our neighbourhood gang would cram
into one car and go to the nearest
hamburger stand for root beer floats –
our finger nails would scrape frost
from the icy mugs as we sipped while
starring at girls wearing shorts
for the first time.

I never dream
        of summer's first BBQs
when the hamburgers would be charred
but pink and juicy inside and
ketchup would drip and stain
my short-sleeved shirt.

Instead
I dream of
        trying to get home
after long weeks of working out-of-town
running to catch the right flight
at the right airport
finding myself confused at the baggage carrousel
watching the circling luggage
hoping to get home in time
for dinner.

Edward A. Tiesse

After Paradise Lost – Elusive Grace[111]

He would sit up high, watch souls as they come –
Thousands and millions, they would cry for love.
Vulgar passion, how Common, how *human*,
He wondered if they knew of Heavn'ly Love –
That breathed him life before the sun could rise,
Love lost in Heav'n he'd never find again,
Love of Beauty, good and ill alike.
A figure, he sleeps and wakes to reminisce.
Yet, he loathes what's made of flesh and bones
Men who throw the name of Love in jest.
Sometimes he'd slither up a tree, a tear
He'd shed and envy lovers' gentle deeds.
For *his* hate for *he* would vain annihilate,
This tender passion is elusive grace.

Bibiana Tsang

The Tesco Lady[112]

My accents speak louder than the words I say. But apparently, not enough
for them to overlook my yellow skin and flat Asian face.

She works at Tesco, didn't even look at me, she sat by the cash-register, high up on her chair –

looked down at me – an incompetent secondary species.
she had that face, like my mother's when I leave dirty dishes in the sink,
dirtier though – because she was not my mother, and my skin was a darker shade.
"F-O-U-R – S-E-V-E-N-T-Y – T-W-O, did you not hear me?" her brows raised and she glared at me.

I don't have much time – I quickly count the pennies and pounds,
the silver ones that are round should be ten pence, or could they be one? Or five? I need a two pence – There was not time to think –
Ah! A 50 pound note! But it only caused trouble.
The lady called for help and they checked the note to make sure it's valid, and I knew:
I was a wealthy Chinese kid who was there to occupy foreign land,
An arrogant invader who ruins the cityscape, who snatches away their bread and milk.

But I've lost my Canto accent. Doesn't that make me worthy?
At school, I was always better because I sound like I grew up speaking the American-British tongue.
Even here, in England, I blend in better than those who speak in their Asian mother tongues.
"Nei mm hai heung gong yan? (Are you not from Hong Kong?)"
But I was. I am.
I just had darker skin, and I was forced to give up my mother tongue.

In Hong Kong, British and American accents signal high education, respectability.
A Chinese accent says, "I am less well educated and I am not worldly."

But when I lost my accent, I felt in the wrong place.
Distanced from my family who did not submit to colonial grace.
I acquired new strength – strength that gave me power and a place
in society.
But I lost a part of me – A set of utterances my parents taught me.

I have lost my accent, but

I am distanced
From
my

root.

Bibiana Tsang

Hunger for Peace of Mind

I hunger for peace, and peace of mind,
But they are now hard to find.
The world has started to go down and down
And each leader acts like a self-promoting clown.
Demonstrators in Hong Kong have made the city
Dangerous and chaotic, which is a great pity,
And many streets are hard to cross
And shopping malls suffer financial loss.
The widespread bushfires way Down Under
Have made the states a smoking wonder
As houses burn and turn to rubbish
And the government's response is weak and snobbish.
But as those fires subside when rain arrives
A virus comes and starts to take many lives.
That virus began in a food market in a city
And the local response was just duplicity,
For the city's officials denied the virus
Could create a global crisis.
But after Wuhan claimed all was fine
The health of the world began to decline
As countries everywhere let their tourists
Spread the disease in cafes, clubs and florists,
Because they had never been warned of the viral dangers
For the Wuhan officials were all free rangers.
And while the virus has infected the world
American politics has fallen as chaos unfurled
As white supremacists do all they can
To support police for killing a black man,
And when thousands line up to demonstrate
The President promises to make America grate.[113]
So while restaurants still serve delicious food
And the fragrance of flowers improves one's mood,
International travel is limited
And families suffer from being separated.
I hunger for peace and freedom, which would revive
The peace of mind we need to survive.

Roger Uren

Desert Island Words[114]

A mere ten to save and savour. Tougher than Discs,
where Ludwig, Wolfgang, Leonard…auto-choose.

Añoranza, the homesickness all we Crusoes suffer,
the Spanish gentler, more heartfelt, not at all bilious.

And **libelula**, Spain's due elegance to the dragon fly,
flameless four-winged ace who mocks the Harrier jet.

France's **Camembert** to allow a laugh on hungry lips:
the perfect cheese…how came it to be a Bert?

Also soft **souvent**, because on my sunburnt skin
often, so often, I'd be trying to recall her touch.

Haiku! I'd jump up and yell to ships on the horizon,
rashly reducing my limited supply to fifteen.

The marvellous **Murrumbidgee** flows 1,485 kms;
a Wiradjuri word English dries to 'plenty of water'.

I might see little **anatroccoli** obedient behind parents,
the Italian for ducklings lingering long on the tongue.

Rome also holds up **aquilone**, the kite I would make
to tug at the heartstrings of not-quite-freedom.

The solid English **steadfast** should check hunger,
loneliness, hold back the temptation to end it all.

Sine qua non, which I'd pronounce both sigh-nigh
and see-nigh. What's 'what-the-heck' in Latin?

A cheat? **Sine qua non** might appear to be three words
but, as with people, without each other they're nothing.

Rod Usher

A Line of Expectations[115]

Too many yeses brought a line of expectations and men to her
door.

Was it her hazel heterochromia, ginger freckles or the stark beauty
of the view from her bedroom window which drew them: Merlins,
red kites, and sometimes peregrine falcons searching for field mice
and rabbits in the rocky green ramble in front of her country
house; she was a generous contrast to the jealous terrain; it took so
much land to graze any livestock. The land itself hungered for her.
She bloomed upon it like dog-rose, Scotch broom or bog-
rosemary. Despite the high ground and wind, sheep would trek up
at day's end and fall asleep standing up.

Too many yeses brought a line of expectations and men to her
door.

The Bible is full of givers and takers, good hearts and bad, of
drunkards and prophets and women who ask for the heads of
saints and fathers who hold knives over the throats of their sons,
imagine voices and ask odd questions of God. Even the wise men
brought incense and myrrh to the baby Jesus she reasoned. She
knew what anyone who sells their time and body knows, it's best to
save for the winters. Her peat moss roof, lambswool blankets and
bosom kept the home warm. Her natural gifts besides her youth,
different coloured eyes, freckles and strawberry hair were simply to
ask and listen. Wives tire of nodding, of holding a prevaricator's
face in their hands, weary of the old excuses, of money squandered
at pubs, of stairs creaking late at night.

Too many yeses brought a line of expectations and men to her
door.

She sold chickens and pies and visits to her secret garden with its
invisible rainbows. Baths were her baptism; her other indulgences:
a small row of leather-bound books and plump Verbena bars of
soap. She was blessed and cursed with no children, but her
barrenness made men hunker down in their woolen coats and hike
in the rain to see her. Her only demands were that they brush their
teeth and bathe before visiting. A few more years and then

freedom from washing sheets each day and hanging them on clotheslines. Perhaps then she would write. But for now:

Too many yeses brought a line of expectations and men to her door.

Peter Coe Verbica

A Typical Modern Chilean Day[116]

It was a typical modern Chilean day:
which chugged through jungle hills like a diesel
until it found us hiding in the little town of Parral.

I had spent the morning measuring
relics of radiation from the Big Bang,

but these were the strangest times,
and due to the shortage of trained doctors,
scientists like me were enlisted to pick up the slack.

We were the front-line soldiers,
tasked with reanimating souls from near death.

Only when a country is truly sick
will you be able to experience the terror of its petty dictators.

I half expected frogs to land
upon our rooftops whenever it rained
and flies to gather like dark clouds.

We washed our hands, threw smocks
over our khakis and donned our masks.

(We did our best to keep bodies
out of the refrigerated trucks
parked in front of the hospital.

I knew the laborers were tired of digging;
I had seen rows of them
lean on their picks and shovels,
as if the tools were all that were holding them upright.)

We were all in this together,
even the musicians who had to leave
their violins in velvet cases

and the women who would sit at the windows
in loose-fitting blouses
with cigarettes in their fingers.

My feet were barking like dogs
when I sat down with my neighbour,
known for his dark eyebrows and

hibernating like the cleverest bear
into the hearts of beautiful women.

Balding, the poet was happiest wearing a hat,
and puffed on a pipe while in his wicker chair.

Though he had been dead for years,
his voice still had a way of sounding out silken syllables:

reminding me of how wealthy men talk to women,
(off handed, friendly and familiar)
as if their audience was filled only
with confidants or concubines.

Fame pursued him like a trotting coyote
after a spotted fawn, and he tired of it,
because it distracted him from his favourite pastime:

writing short poems about his past infidelities
which he would pull line by line
from the carved rosewood box
of his mind.

Despite being a Communist,
he knew the cut of a good suit,
but the late afternoon was still too hot today for that.

His jacket slung over the back of his chair
and a map of perspiration
ran down the side of his shirt

like a thin country hugging a fat continent.

"Silly to think that we have been
at war for years over who first came up
with the pisco sour," he said.

It was good to hear a man
who could write about the universe
in a lover's eye
also discuss something so inane and simple,

on a typical modern Chilean day.

Peter Coe Verbica

"I thought I told them for you"[117]

"I thought I told them for you."
Her eyes water as they grow, larger than they should, soon
they'll swallow her face.

They keep growing, wider than a bullfrog's extended throat.
I hear her voice crack and picture a pond, serene, reflective
croaking.

It's unsettling. I'm afraid they'll pop, pop and swallow
her face. Pop and cover her in gelatinous ooze that looks
stickier than it is. Like boiled fish eyes,
rich in vitamins, but swollen soft, distended.

My aunt's family is Iqaluit, when they eat seal
the heart goes to the youngest and the eyes to the sickest,
because that's where the nutrients are, the iron and ore.
The strength.

"I'm not angry. I understand."
I mean to say it loud enough for her to hear. Confident enough
that she'll believe me,
but I'm barely whispering, and she's angry.
"Stop lying to me! If you're angry just fucking say so. It's better
than this, this, fucking silence."
She only swears when she's doesn't know what to say. She told me
so
as we were leaving an exhibition of her father's work,
"Fuckin' Hell." she gripped my bicep, "I know too much
to comment on it. I've only fucks and hells. Abject and abscess."

Her eyes are larger than my fists, heavier than a march, beating
down on me; two one two, for Christ's sake! Close
those exaggerated lumps of soul, of vitamins, of iron rich jelly,
those seal-fat fucking vitamin eyes
even one would do, I've been sick for too long, please,
just pluck it out
feed it to me.

But she's on her knees, ear pressed against the space
under the door, jaw locked.
And then I'm following her; out a window,
down a fire escape, further still.

Sarah Vetter

Whaea[118]

Shines so bright she can clearly see and be seen.

A wahine warrior, fearless and mighty.

Her light shines through the whitest of the long white clouds of
Aotearoa.

Her heart beckons a ray of sunshine and she is followed;

this wahine my dearest is in the right waka.

She is adored for her kindness and wisdom;

a pillar of strength to hold on to.

Her purpose is clear and bountiful –

tangata whenua and pakeha united in kai. –

Aroha is her waiata.

Steadfast the wahine call for this generation in time of change.

A rangatira for all! A priceless taonga.

Renee Wade

Eating for One[119]

Sardines are sold in flat tins.
Sealed. Airtight. Coffined.
To prepare a simple meal,
put a finger in the ring. Pull.
Headless fish, gossamer skin.
Quiet and slim, like me.
Lift the frail bodies. Free
the fine chain-links of bone.
They smell of the seaside,
reddish flesh like rain on clay.
Tins are self-contained,
sustaining, easily shelved.
I'm the Tin Woman,
probing a sardine heart.

Victoria Walvis

It is Spider Season[120]

in Mui Wo, where a smiling stranger told me how
during the Great Leap Forward, neighbours swapped
children. And ate them. He said that spider babies
cling to a mother's back. She eats what she sees.

I hiked in striking heat under the gossamer traps
to the hum of cicadas, a song parched and dying
like land in Egypt. Dot, under naked, hungry sky.
The kids on the beach made me sick, and now

the cows shit in the road, swaying tails at dusk.
Grounded. It is almost like joy to gulp a beer
on the pier-side, fairyland, belly fed, watching boats
sit so close to water, they are almost drowning.

Victoria Walvis

The Harbour Swimmer[121]

Left, right. Left, right. Breathe.

You are hard boiled candy, or salted caramel,
or liquid light between two not-so-ancient stones,
their limpets packed like flats in built up places.

Splash, splash. Splash, splash. Pause.

The swash and wash of quiet eddies against
the wall where I'm watching the harbour, sweating like
an egg that someone cracked and left to spoil.

Not the city heaving its shell past the molten rush of noon.
Not the brave boys, shirtless to the day, playing basketball.
Not the Sunday women, chatting in shaded places.

You are not part of this. Oblivious to the scum and stink,
the soggy plastic, you switch freely to breaststroke.
Tiny dancer before the white flags of big ships.

Arms out and back. Out and back.
To the concealed heart.

You glide through froth and oil, striking neatly
like a kite will in a certain wind. And hidden stars
throw down tears to lodge in wave dimples.

The old face is wrinkled, winking as though
you might swim in the furrows forever.
The water never asks us what we are.

Victoria Walvis

Before and after

A plunge into the dark hole
Reluctantly or willingly
A cry greeted with happiness or disappointment

Chubby limbs, pink faces
Shouting
One word, two words, three words
Broken sentence, one sentence, two sentences
More

Skinny limbs, wrinkled faces
Murmuring
Two sentences, one sentence, broken sentence
Three words, two words, one word
None

A breath into the bright light
Reluctantly or willingly
A silence accompanied with gaiety or sadness

Honghua Wang

Courage

A box of chilled chicken cage bone
from Market Place
with chicken-feet missing

I wonder how this chicken can be so courageous
Fleeing the town overnight
Such a foresight!

I wonder the route he took.

Obviously not through Tolo Harbour
Though he could fly a little bit,
he might not be able to dodge man-made UFOs

Obviously not through Tai Chung Kiu Road
The heat and smoke!
Definitely he could not stand

Obviously, he had found a short-cut
awaiting our discovery

Anyway, he made it
even without a diploma

What he needed was
COURAGE and
DETERMINATION
I guess

Honghua Wang

Fight

Caught by us one day,
On the floor, you panicked.
Challenging the ownership and
Kicking off the fight, you sought to
Reunite with your hibernating family.
Over and over, we were annoyed;
Again and again, we were troubled.
Comfort abandons us with you
Hiding in books, rice bags and fridge and giving us no clue.

Honghua Wang

Lost

Aw
Rder
Ympathy
Olerance

Honghua Wang

apresurándose, no[122]

If there were no palms dropping fronds
in the breeze like a royal trail to Jerusalem
and if la lingua met el agua y la fortuna
and found nothing but beans and rice and
if el amor del dinero was just another way
to spell a part of a meal and money passed
like sinners in the night and if every
inflection of el idioma spelled more than
the sum of its letters and they were less
numb at the prospect of any of kind of split
if the only way to find myself was to jump ship
into the deepest seas and if there was a way
to know what it would feel like without ever
leaving the white sand beaches of Puerto Rico
and if my shade was two years darker than it had
been before and the door to this place was two feet
wider and if I never felt like I would need to hide
and my soul could be seen in every café con leche
without a worry of apresurándose under the sun
then I could understand the finality of un concepción
y nada me alejaría de la alegría

Bruce Arlen Wasserman

Death

After the sale of the house & its empty space
after the pain of your last minutes burned into
my senses like a calf branding chanting the fact
that dying is forever & after that, I sit down
in your favourite place but don't order what you
always ate & the sinking lime pit of my insides is
a slough of feelings I may never sort, may never
put to voice even as a slow dirge pipes your casket
to its final hole in the dirt, and this is why letters will
find their place in words and this is why breathing still
works when it's short and sharp and this is why your
eyes' glazed looks those last 5 minutes of eternity filled
every bit of blood that spit up its soul, & even if there was
a way to smooth it all like an oil slicked skin & even if
the voices drown out my thoughts & even if the child in me
wants to close his eyes so that it will all fall away then rise
with a spark like before, these things will not suffice,
though maybe time will erase itself like threads of chalk
on a board once black but then finally faded grey.

Bruce Arlen Wasserman

After the Storm and the Flood[123]

I'm in deep, deep waters sinking,
swimming in lead, pressing, pressing.
A salamander with shark's teeth
bites his way through a sunken harp.
Glued to a golden throne, Canute
sits with plump Kardashian lips,
gurgling out "I do like to be
beside the Seaside. I do like
to be beside the sea." I know

you are there on the surface above,
waiting, waiting, becalmed and calm
as after every storm, scanning
the flat, gray expanse of a smooth sea
for a hint or a hope of the former me.

But I'm not coming, coming back.
Nine nodding shipwrecked nuns are here
cooking on the floor of the deep,
such fine fare. They hold and lock
aromas in bubbles. Keep watch,
keep watch, for they will soar up,
and near you on a sociable wave they'll stop,
then playfully burst in a cool, pellucid pop.

George Watt

An Embarrassment of Pleasure[124]

He sits atop a pointless flight of steps
that run down the muddy side of the gorge
right into the river. He can't be clearly seen
with the low sun behind him. Arms raised, his song
or prayer fills the gully, then runs with the river

all the way to the sea. A thin, primrose, late-day light
softens everything hard and all rough textures.
I imagine with muddy legs, runny noses
invisible children's calls and laughter
insinuate their way into the lines of his song.

And on my side of the river beside the path,
camellia branches fill a huge dented drum,
the blooms blood-red against cool metallic grey.
There's a shaky scrawl on a rough card
tucked into this bright, cheerful free-for-all.

"Help yourself! But please, don't take too much."

George Watt

The Blackbirds of Cooper Place[125]

for Jessie 1924-2018

"Doesn't she look beautiful." No. She's yellow,
gray, skeletal, a corpse. Dead. Just. Dead.
Run, run from Rest in Peace *et al.*
The blackbirds too look lost. Who will sweep up
the mess left on the long path to the road:
the price of worms; the price of song?
Twice a day she'd sweep it back to the beds,
but they'd wait in the jacaranda tree
or the ancient pepper tree, till she turned
her back, and they'd drop and scatter again.
On still, warm nights we'd sit on the deck
hoping the mosquitoes would stay away,
and sure enough the plaintive song would come,
notes hanging in the calm evening air.
If you could you'd grab them, hold them, we would.
Instead, we try to find her location, pin her
down, and just as we think she's there or there
her notes rise from another place. The song
is never quite the same: shadows alter,
a cricket might chirrup, or my chair creak
when trying not to make a human sound.
Now when the blackbirds sing at Cooper Place
you will not be there listening, but I can't escape
the notion that you are there, inside their song,
part of their love of evening and joy in spring.
Oh I don't know of a heaven, but do know this:
we three are infinitesimal notes that join
a great chorus, the Music of the Spheres,
and its baffling harmony, no beginning no end.
But for now, coda, I'll go and sweep the path.

George Watt

Empty[126]

I'm sitting alone on a long low bench,
my new schoolbag on an uncertain lap.
Just five years old. Waiting. Shuffling. Sighing.
Mustard walls are thick with overpainting,
cheerful enough against red locker doors.
Staring at row upon row of black hooks
high up, for big boys and girls. Hooks waiting too,
curling for want of jackets or shirts or stuff.
The room holds its breath, eager for chatter
and children to fill it up, make moisture
that runs down high windows of frosted glass.
On this first day at school, having nothing
to do and must do something, I slowly
unwind two thick leather straps from buckles,
brass buckles, colder than the day allows.
    Unused to handling, the straps rasp and squeak,
complaining at the undoing. The bag's flap creaks
open. Oh the rich, thick smell of leather,
a genie out with magic to mix with Dettol
hints in the air. A bag like a room needs filling.
But with what? Books certainly, but more than that:
discoveries, loves, joys, dismays, things, terrors.
They have everything to do with an empty bag,
and a waiting boy. And within hearing,
an oncoming approach of voices, muffles, shuffles,
from a long line of children. So the bag
must now be buckled up quickly, with a sigh,
to preserve its secrets from inquisitive eyes.

George Watt

Hunger

Hunger, intrinsic, essential
feeling we must have
to sustain life, survive.
Hunger must be fed relentlessly,
kept alive, demanding.

When hunger strikes,
in forms unimaginable,
panic is unstoppable,
we must eat to survive!

Yet, there is a hunger
meaning more than survival:
hunger for knowledge
keeps us on this planet
while we look beyond.

Hunger – means we yearn
Hunger – means we strive
Hunger – means we are alive.

Mocco Wollert

Hunger – Power

The rat in the stomach
has teeth that gnaw,
rip, spread pain
without pity or relief.

Bloated stomachs
look like storage tanks
filled with food.

They are
silent screams,
extending, they beg,
implore to be fed.

Hollow eye sockets
speak of hunger
in a universal language.

Hunger is a force
without compassion, mercy;
it overpowers education,
scruples, morals, ethics.

Only love has the strength
to withstand hunger,
to rather die than give in.

Mocco Wollert

HUNGER
Acrostic

H – Humiliation – begs – breaks the spirit

U – Understand – first step to eradicate hunger

N – Neglect – cause of extended bellies, stick limbs

G – Generations – lost forever through starvation

E – Emergency – mankind screams for sustenance

R – Rejection – ignores uncomfortable truth

Mocco Wollert

To Hunger for Righteousness[127]

A call to arms!
To hunger for righteousness.
A call to arms!
To fight injustices.
With all our might,
We will defend the feeble.
We'll do what's right
For the good of the people.

There are those
Who sulk in silent anger.
There are those
Distressed by deaths from hunger.
Let's do what we should
To uphold our values dear.
Let's do what we could
Not awed or dismayed by fear.

We'll overcome
Despite the gnawing pain.
We'll overcome
For love and not for gain.
We are not flabbergasted;
Our will won't flag or bend!
All evil will be blasted;
Glory is ours in the end!

Elizabeth (Libby) Wong

Throne of Thorns

You compare me to roses
To her beautiful blooms,
her elegant hues,
her feminine floral aromas of youth.

Then you started picking me apart
One by one in the name of "love"
Until you reached a dozen,
Too excited to reveal your grand romantic gesture to notice your
vice-like grip and the crimson dripping from your fingertips.

You wait for my declaration of adoration with a smug smirk and a
glint in your eye until you realize I'm too preoccupied with trying
not to cry.
You could't understand why.
And that's when you saw red.
You rip each and every petal off, seething.
Obscenities of every kind pouring, overflowing.
Your bloody hand grips the naked stems and throws them to the
ground like they're nothing.
Like they're nothing.
But they're everything.
They're all I've ever known.
And without my petals, what am I?
Just thorns?

Thorns.
Roses aren't roses without their thorns.
And that realization shocked me to my core.
For upon these thorns I shall build my throne.
I will rise and grow again.
I will unleash my allure unabashedly.
I will embody my femininity fiercely.

Yes, I am beautiful and elegant and still somewhat naive.
Yes, I have faults and insecurities all spread out for you to see.
But resilience and determination runs through my veins and resides
in my seeds.

Watch me conquer the trauma and all of the pain you left me.
I'm stronger than ever, I'm no longer the same.
For upon these thorns I will build my throne.
Because I am a rose.
And roses have thorns.

Wan-Ting (Joyce) Wu

Asylum in Happy Meals[128]

home
where golden arcs light up, overarching
where you forge a fort on stiff benches
laying all of you for a lavish pause
where people grill in reverie
crackling sizzling scrumptious heaps
where you convince yourself, seeing is eating
where it was either a flea cage or a table on which
dried ketchup does not concede
where mites shall not suck malnourished blood
where you hold on to your skin ravenously
aware of the foreignness of ground meat
where the freshness of iceberg lettuce
sprinkles on your worn-out ear
where casually dripped soft serve
sends succulence up your chin
where grease patches soak through
scraps of burnt chips
where asylum is in happy meals –
while at the same time someone takes it
home,

just for a midnight snack.

Wing Chit Yung

Infection control[129]

Once magma breaks the crust,
It is no longer a vessel for tectonic plates
Lava flows, destroying what it sees
Once phlegm leaves the airway,
It is no longer a nuisance to the throat
Sputum gets screwed into vials immediately
A biohazard.

In the lab everything is treated as contagion
Everything is universal, all matter:
That swab? Flame it.
                    That hand? Scrub it raw.
Turn on the laundry machine and let
Aerosol swirl above the boiling point
Where dirtiness sent from the dirty team
Dies in minutes because no one should breathe
Suctioned by negative pressure rooms
A burning suffocation.

But a sneeze was not a volcanic eruption
Before; all we know is somewhere in a stone cave,
It lay dormant, waiting only for one naive person
to spread it on villages in front of their mouths.

Wing Chit Yung

Voices of rain[130]

Sand slithers from their hands
Raw material for glass
Sharp wedges of curved necks
Splattered on bricks replaced by tar

Or, the weighing of demerara
Recipe for sweet, sweet crumbles
Draws plumes on their faces
Eat it, the dessert you deserve

Like deafening hands flapping
Around red in the People's hall
How its uniformity must have
Triggered earthquakes at some point

And maybe, maybe
They were merely sounds of amber rain
On a regular June, longing eyes
Precipitating stubborn moisture
In the free-flowing air.

Wing Chit Yung

THE POETS

The following brief biographies are based on texts provided by the poets. As there is an interval of months between the submission of brief biographies and the editing of the Anthology, much may have changed in the meantime.

VINITA AGRAWAL is the author of four books of poetry – *Two Full Moons* (Bombaykala Books), *Words Not Spoken* (Brown Critique), *The Longest Pleasure* (Finishing Line Press) and *The Silk Of Hunger* (AuthorsPress) – Vinita is a Mumbai based, award winning poet and writer. She was Senior Editor with Womaninc.com for three years. Recipient of the Rabindranath Tagore Literary Prize 2018, Gayatri GaMarsh Memorial Award for Literary Excellence, USA, 2015, her poems have appeared in *Asiancha, Constellations, The Fox Chase Review, Pea River Journal, Lumen, Cyclamen And Swords, Open Road Review, Stockholm Literary Review, Poetry Pacific, Mithila Review, Chandrabhaga, Blue Fifth Review, The Bombay Review* and other journals and in anthologies from Australia, Ireland and Israel. She was nominated for the Best of the Net Awards in 2011. Her poem won a prize for the Moon Anthology on the Moon by TallGrass Writers Guild 2017. She was awarded first prize in the Wordweavers Contest 2014, commendation prize in the All India Poetry Competition 2014. She contributed a monthly column on Asian Poets on the literary blog of the Hamline university, Saint Paul, USA in 2016-17. She judged the RLFPA poetry contest (International Prize) in 2016 and co-judged *Asian Cha*'s poetry contest on The Other Side, in 2015. She has read at the FILEY Book Fair, Merida, Mexico, Kala Ghoda Arts Festival, Lucknow Literary festival, Cappuccino Readings and Women Empowerment events. She is on the Advisory Board of the Tagore Literary Prize. She co-curates events for PEN Mumbai and sub-curates for the Kala Ghoda Literary Festival.

JOY AL-SOFI is a published writer of poetry, fiction and non-fiction. She was a Third-Winner in the Inaugural Proverse Poetry Competition. Originally from the USA, where she was a practicing attorney, she has been teaching English in Hong Kong since 2004. Her latest passion is photographing butterflies and other Hong Kong wildlife.

SHIKHA BANSAL has worked in the publishing industry for several years. She lives in Hong Kong.

ALAN BERN is a recently retired Children's Librarian from the Berkeley Public Library. He worked in public libraries in the San Francisco Bay Area for over 25 years in a variety of jobs. He is a poet, storywriter, and photographer and has two books of poetry published by Fithian Press: *No no the saddest* (2004) and *Waterwalking in Berkeley* (2007). A third book of poetry, *greater distance and other poems* (2015), was published by his own press, Lines & Faces, a press and publisher specializing in illustrated poetry broadsides, collaborating with the artist Robert Woods, linesandfaces.com. Alan was a runner up for The Raw Art Review's The John H. Kim Memorial Short Fiction Prize for his story 'The alleyway near the downtown library'; and he won a medal from SouthWest Writers for his story 'The Return of the Very Fierce Wolf of Gubbio to Assisi, 1943 CE [and now, 2013 CE].' He was also a finalist in the NCWN's 2019 Thomas Wolfe Fiction Prize; he won the Littoral Press Poetry Prize in 2015; and he was a semi-finalist in the 2016 Center for the Book Arts Poetry Chapbook Competition. Alan has poems, stories, and photos published in a wide variety of online and print publications, from which his work has been nominated for Pushcart Prizes. Alan is also a performer working with the dancer Lucinda Weaver as PACES: dance & poetry fit to the space and with musicians from Composing Together,
http://composingtogether.org/index.php/programs/
http://composingtogether.org/index.php/sample-poetry-from-our-musical-storytime-performances/

THEA BIESHEUVEL is currently a resident of Australia, although born in the Netherlands. It took a while to master the English language but I now have four publications to my name. My passion is poetry but short stories come a close second. I can be found in a Google search or in Smashwords and other on-line publications.

LIAM BLACKFORD is an Australian living in Hong Kong.

MARÍA ELENA BLANCO (Havana, Cuba) Poet, essayist and translator, writes predominantly in her native Spanish. Having spent a good part of her formative years in New York, she translates her own poetry into English and has also developed her own English poetic voice in a style quite distinguishable from her Spanish one. Has taught French literature and language and worked for the United Nations as translator/reviser, presently on a freelance basis. She is a frequent participant in international literary events and a member of Labyrinth, the Association of English-Speaking Poets in Vienna. Her published work includes poetry collections *Posesión por pérdida* (Sevilla and

Santiago, Chile, 1990), *Corazón sobre la tierra / tierra en los Ojos* (Cuba, 1998), *Alquímica memoria* (Madrid, 2001), *Mitologuías* (Madrid, 2001), *danubiomediterráneo /mittelmeerdonau* (Vienna, 2005, Spanish-German), *El amor incontable* (Madrid, 2008), *Havanity / Habanidad* (Miami, 2010, English-Spanish), *Escrito en lenguas* (Chile, 2015), *Sobresalto al vacío* (Chile, 2015), *Botín* (Leiden, 2016) and *Oro vano* (Chile, 2018), as well as a book of literary criticism, *Asedios al texto literario* (Madrid, 1999), and a volume of critical essays on Cuban culture and politics, *Devoraciones. Ensayos de período especial* (Leiden, 2016). She has also published Spanish translations of French and Austrian poets. She shares her time between her home in Vienna (Austria), Chile, and the Andalusian countryside.

GAVIN BOURKE has worked in public service for over twenty years. He grew up in the suburb of Tallaght, in West Dublin and lives in County Meath. He holds a B.A. in Humanities from Dublin City University, an M.A. Degree in Modern Drama Studies and a Higher Diploma in Information Studies, from University College Dublin. His work broadly covers, nature, time, memory, addiction, mental health, human relationships, the inner and outer life, creating meaning and purpose, politics, contemporary and historical social issues, injustice, the human situation, power and its abuse, as well as urban and rural life, personal autonomy, ethics, in English and to a lesser extent, in the Irish Language. He has participated in many national and international poetry competitions, with both single poems and book-length collections, winning some and being shortlisted and/or highly commended in others. He has been published internationally in various literary journals and has participated in literary festivals. Gavin is also a multi-instrumentalist and has been a songwriter and composer for the past thirty years.

LAWRENCE BRIDGES In America, Lawrence Bridges is best known for work in the film and literary world. His poetry has appeared in *The New Yorker*, *Poetry*, *The Tampa Review*, and *Ambit*. He has published three volumes of poetry, *Horses on Drums*, *Flip Days*, and *Brownwood*. He created a series of literary documentaries for the National Endowment for the Arts 'Big Read' initiative, which includes profiles of Ray Bradbury, Amy Tan, Tobias Wolff and Cynthia Ozick. He lives in Los Angeles.

PAUL BROOKE's poetry has been in such journals as the *North American Review*, *The Antioch Review*, *International Poetry Review*, *Isotope: A Journal of Literary Nature and Science Writing*, and the *Interdisciplinary Study of Literature and the Environment*.

He is the author of four full-length poetry collections: *Light and Matter: Photographs and Poems of Iowa* (2008), *Meditations on Egrets: Photographs and Poems of Sanibel* (2010), *Sirens and Seriemas: Photographs and Poems of the Amazon and Pantanal* (2015) and *Arm Wrestling at the Iowa State Fair* (2018). His most recent book is *Jaguars of the Northern Pantanal: Panthera onca at the Meeting of the Waters* (2020).

Dr Brooke is a Professor of English Grand View University in Des Moines, Iowa, where he teaches Advanced Creative Writing, Introduction to Creative Writing, Environmental Literature and Literary Theory. He was trained as an undergraduate as an ornithologist and later completed his Bachelors and Masters at Iowa State University and his Ph.D. in English at the University of Nebraska-Lincoln.

LINA BUIVIDAVICIUTE was born on May 14, 1986. She has a BA in Lithuanian philology and advertising, and a MA in Lithuanian literature. She is a poet, literary scholar and literary critic. Her first poetry book *Helsinki Syndrome* was published in 2017.

PAOLA CARONNI hails from Italy and has been living in Asia for over twenty years. She resides now in Hong Kong, where she is a translator, interpreter and tutor of Italian language. Paola holds an MFA in Creative Writing from the University of Hong Kong and an MA in English Language and Literature from the University of Milan.

Paola is the Vice-Director and editor of the online lifestyle and culture magazine *Ciao Magazine* (www.ciaomag.com). Paola's poems have been published in the printed anthologies: *Desde Hong Kong: Poets in Conversation with Octavio Paz, Quixotica: Poems East of La Mancha, Mingled Voices* (Vols 2, 3 and 4); and *Poems from the Lockdown*. Other poems have appeared among others, in *Voice and Verse Poetry Magazine, Cha, an Asian Literary Journal, New Asian Writing, From Whispers to Roars, Fearsome Critters*. Paola's fiction has appeared on *Pen-Hong Kong*.

Paola writes that she is a very active poet in the local Hong Kong scene. She helps organising special poetry nights, takes part in readings, and regularly attends Poetry Nights.

Paola explores the struggle and displacement of coming from the West but belonging to the East. Her poetry often focuses on the unique sights, sounds, and smells of the Far East, on the recent changes and turmoil happening in Hong Kong, and on the feeling of longing for Italy, a country undergoing political and social transformations.

VINCENT CASAREGOLA teaches American literature and film, creative writing, rhetorical studies, and composition. He has published poetry in a number of journals, including *The Bellevue Review*, *The Examined Life*, *Natural Bridge*, WLA, *Dappled Things*, *2River*, *Work*, *Lifelines*, and *Blood and Thunder*. He has also published creative nonfiction and flash fiction.

ANNE CASEY is an award-winning Sydney-based Irish poet/writer and author of two collections published by Salmon Poetry – *out of emptied cups* (2019) and *where the lost things go* (2017). A journalist, magazine editor, legal author and media communications director for 30 years, her work ranks in leading national daily newspaper, *The Irish Times'* Most Read, and is widely published and anthologised internationally – The Irish Poetry Reading Archive (James Joyce Library, University College Dublin), *The Irish Times*, *The Canberra Times*, *Beltway Poetry Quarterly*, *Tahoma Literary Review*, *Australian Poetry Anthology*, *Quiddity*, *Entropy*, *apt*, *The Murmur House*, *Barzakh*, DASH, *The Stony Thursday Book*, *FourXFour*, *Westerly Magazine*, *Cordite Poetry Review*, *Verity La*, *Mingled Voices 4* and *Plumwood Mountain Review* among many others. Anne has won or been shortlisted for prizes in Ireland, Northern Ireland, the UK, the USA, Canada, Hong Kong and Australia, and serves on numerous literary advisory boards.

IAN CHAMBERS was born to working-class parents in post-war Manchester, England. His modest ancestry includes an illegitimate parent and grandparent, a possible Dublin prostitute and illiterate farm labourers in Ireland's Great Famine. His Dublin-born mother managed the office of the small firm where his orphanage-raised father worked as a printer. When Ian was five years old the family emigrated to Australia as 'Ten Pound Poms'. The long sea voyage, exotic ports of call and pioneering spirit of their new homeland had a profound impact. Ian attempts to capture thoughts, experiences, emotions and observations through poetry much as one uses a camera to capture a visual record – "a photograph can capture what you saw at a specific instant but poetry can relate so much more". With the apparent dichotomy between his Irish Catholic roots and his scientific training, particularly in light of emotional family misfortunes (his father suffered from Parkinson's and his mother from Alzheimer's), the themes of mortality and purpose feature prominently in his poetry – "I think most of us would like to feel that there's a point to our existence. For many, religion satisfies that desire, but many others must try to reconcile the incomprehensible complexity, vastness, power and beauty of the universe with the apparent insignificance and futility of human life". Private travels and an exciting career have taken him all over the world and exposed him to numerous cultures. He has lived in the UK, Australia, France, The Netherlands, Oman and the USA. Now retired, he lives in Ireland. Ian has an honours degree in astrophysics from London University and Master's degrees in computer systems management from Maryland University and international relations from Cambridge. He is a fellow of the RSA and the BCS.

JOSIE CHAMBERS lives and works in the UK. She is currently Development Fellow of the Comino Foundation, an educational charity. Previously she held the role of Assistant Vice-Chancellor at the University of Winchester, where she was a Professor of Organisational Learning, working mainly with organisations in the public sector. In 2011 she was awarded the MBE in the Queen's Birthday Honours, for services to Higher Education. When invited, she shares her poems with friends, colleagues and wider audiences. In 2019, a collection of her poems – *This Good Fight* – was published by The Choir Press. *This Good Fight* offers a loose narrative, settling on moments in the joys and struggles which, in different guises, underpin human life.

KRISHNA CHAMLING, aka, Kr. Chamling grew up in the countryside and is a lecturer and poet writing in the English language from Kathmandu, the capital city of Nepal. He is English department Chief at K & K. International College, and advisor for the National Institute for Career Development (NICD) in Kathmandu.

He has been involved in various private academic organizations, serving as an English language instructor for IELTS and TOEFL, as Motivator and Trainer for local social development programmes for young guns through a Community Development Organization, (MH) Media House, (NICD) National Institute for Career Development in Kathmandu, Nepal.

Through his poetry, he wants to engender consciousness and contribute awareness, insight and aspiration in the minds of readers, as well as in the public sphere, for better understanding of the human psyche, which will hopefully lead towards an optimistic future for the world.

He is widely known poet among readers in the world's most popular poetic groups on face book.

JESSICA CHAN (b. 1997) is a writer of poems and short stories. Her works have been published in various publications such as Voice & Verse Poetry Magazine. She is a recipient of a Hong Kong Top Story Award in 2012 and 2014 and has been longlisted twice in the Tower Poetry competition. She is currently studying a MSt in Creative Writing at the University of Cambridge. Born and raised in Hong Kong, she divides her time between Hong Kong and London.

KWAN EE CHAN, TOM, "holds an MFA in Creative Writing at the University of Hong Kong, where he also holds his BA in Language and Communication. He is a poet and short story writer and his poems have published in *Voice & Verse Poetry Magazine* and *Cha: An Asian Literary Journal*. He also published his first book, *The Twelve Chimes Before Christmas*, under the pseudonym Orion Blightman, in January 2018. Inspired by the works of Raymond Carver, Tom is currently writing a short story collection set in the carnivalesque city of Hong Kong."

CAROL FLAKE CHAPMAN is a former journalist. She returned to poetry, her first love, after the sudden death of her husband on a wild river in Guatemala shattered her world. Poetry, she found, was the language she needed not only for healing but to respond to a troubled world. Since then, she has performed her poems at gatherings around the world, and her poems have been published in numerous anthologies.

CHENG TIM TIM is a secondary school teacher. Her poems have been published in *Cha: An Asian Literary Journal*, *SAND* Journal, *Cordite Poetry Review*, among others. She is one of the co-founding editors of EDGE: HKBU Creative Journal.

ANNIE CHRISTAIN is an associate professor of composition and ESOL at SUNY Cobleskill and a former artist resident of the Shanghai Swatch Art Peace Hotel and the Arctic Circle Art and Science Expedition. Her poems have appeared in *Seneca Review*, *Oxford Poetry*, *Prelude*, and *The Lifted Brow*, among others. She was a winner of the Driftwood Press In-House Poem Contest and received the grand prize of the Hart Crane Memorial Poetry Contest, the Greg Grummer Poetry Award, the Oakland School of the Arts Enizagam Poetry Award, and the Neil Shepard Prize in Poetry. *Tall As You Are Tall Between Them,* her debut book of poetry, was published by C&R Press.

WILLIAM LEO COAKLEY's poems have been published for many years in magazines, anthologies, and newspapers here and abroad (including China, England, and Ireland). He often gives public readings, especially at the Poetry Society in London and the Leslie-Lohman Museum of Art and the Irish American Writers and Artists theatre in New York and on the radio in Montreal and Boston.

His poems have won awards in the Arvon Foundation Sotheby's International Poetry Competition in England, the Yeats Society in New York, and the New England Poetry Club.

For the last two years in Ireland (where he is also a citizen) he has been on the shortlist for the New Irish Writing Prize, with the selected poems being published in the *Irish Times*.

SUZANNE COTTRELL, an Ohio buckeye by birth, lives with her husband and two rescued dogs in rural Piedmont North Carolina. An outdoor enthusiast and retired history and special education teacher, she enjoys reading, writing, hiking, knitting, Pilates, Tai Chi, and yoga. She enjoys nature's sensory stimuli and making associations between human beings and the natural world. Her poems have appeared in numerous journals and anthologies including *Best Emerging Poets Series*, *Avocet*, *Poetry Quarterly*, *Plum Tree Tavern*, *The Pangolin Review*, *The Scarlet Leaf Review*, and *Burningword Literary Journal*. She was the recipient of the 2017 Rebecca Lard Poetry Award, Prolific Press.

NEIL DOUGLAS is a poet/doctor from the United Kingdom currently working in Community Paediatrics in London's East End. He is an enthusiastic member of the Covent Garden Stanza affiliated with the Poetry Society and has published work in the UK, North America and Hong Kong.

GAYATHRI DURAIRAJ is a writer, poet, global nomad and also an economist who has published in a variety of magazines and has run a writers club in American school of Bombay from 2016 to 2018. There she has spearheaded three anthologies for the school. Her first book of poems titled, *Quintessential Me*, was published in June 2018 and she is currently working on her second one based on the city of Mumbai. She finds pleasure in the simplest of things and derives inspiration for her writing from her many travels and experiences. She is fondly known as 'Gaya'.

AHMED ELBESHLAWY is the author of *America in Literature and Film* (Routledge), *Woman in Lars von Trier's Cinema* (Palgrave), *Twenty-Five Meditations on Writing and Subjectivity* (London Academic Publishing) and the poetry collection *Savage Charm* (Proverse Hong Kong).

RAYN EPREMIAN is a poet, filmmaker, and writer of fantasy novels, science fiction screenplays, and the occasional musical. She currently resides in Edinburgh, Scotland.

D. W. EVANS was born in Newcastle upon Tyne. First study, then work took him south to London, then Brighton and eventually Jersey. 'Discharged Wednesday' won the Alan Jones Memorial Prize 2019. 'Rapunzel' was selected for a prize and appeared in *A3 Review* (April 2020 edition). La Rue des Touettes was shortlisted for the 7th Ó Bhéal Five Words Poetry Competition, and published in *Five Words*, Vol. XIII. 'Turnips' was, highly commended in the first Acumen International Poetry Competition 2019/20.

ADELE EVERSHED is originally from Wales. She has lived in both Hong Kong and Singapore before settling in Connecticut USA. Adele has only recently turned her hand to writing poetry. She likes to write verse influenced by her experience of living in different countries and has poetry published by Didcot Writers and the journal, *Three Drops From A Cauldron*. Adele has had her flash fiction stories published by a variety of online journals. She recently was a semi-finalist in the London Independent Story Project competition and has had a story featured in the anthology, *Museum*, published by Enliven Press.

RYAN FENTON grew up in the United States, and he now lives in Hong Kong.

DANIELA FISCHEROVÁ was born in 1948 in Prague. She is a playwright, novelist, screenwriter, poet, children's author (IBBY – International Board on Books for Young People – 2016 Honours List). Wife, mother, grandmother.

LINCOLN GREENHAW for the last five years lived in Beirut, Lebanon and Guangzhou, China before settling down to write in Silver Spring, Maryland. He holds an MFA in poetry from Colorado State University. His work has been featured in *The Ishaan Review* and *Jacket2*.

CASEY HAMPTON is a poet and fiction writer currently residing in the Pacific Northwest. His work has appeared in *Dialogue*, *Entropy*, *Star 82 Review*, *Euphony Journal* and elsewhere. When not writing, he helps out on the family farm and spends as much time as he can with his coonhound Josie.

MATTHEW SCOTT HARRIS "This introductory pseudo bio iz chess a (brief once a pawn nah time) knight errant blurb hash tagged off from thy secluded posh bishopric....

"He got born in Cincinnati that buckeye state. January 13th MCMLIX marked his initial years to date. A tangle of arms & legs testing lungs, which sounded great. He kind of resembled a misshapen octopus with oval pate. Glowering inxs of deep purple from blue mood being irate. Thrust out the womb of Harriet Harris whom Boyce did date. After courting this youngest Kuritsky kin after whose near half century marriage cursed ill-fate. Whisked by grim reaper, which demise she did hate. For her being imbued with vim and vinegar til illness ate.

"Away her je nais sais quois personable maternal trait. Evident during my boyhood reflected by her son of late. As he too inches closer to his mortality and Hades gate.

"tis a field day to jerry rig a king's ransom, asper communicating, expressing, gut heaving input kindle ling my outlook per questionable rite Trump violated with yipping brigands doing dirty deeds done dirt cheap.

"though unknown to thee reading public and chattering class, this totally tubular thought provoking meister jabberwocky houses full deshabille attire invoking an automatic repulsion.

"no ambition to clothe himself in the latest fashion alway found this middle aged, monkey, mwm to be an outlier. early years of mine kempf fraught with emotional, physical and spiritual angst, when forced thru the gauntlet thrown up by punks.

"they throve on being mean, and stepped up the propensity of bullying, especially since this presently grown man evinced an extremely cowering, frowning, identity guard.

"one solid punch (encouraged by me late mum, this before the onset of safe zones from raging red bulls verbally warbling denigrating, howling, insidious malicious quanta vile zeal."

KATE HAWKINS is a TV presenter, actress and writer in Hong Kong and Australia. Having grown up between the two countries she has found writing a source of great importance in understanding and contemplating the richness of her life. This is the sixth anthology her work has been published in and she has also edited two anthologies for the Hong Kong Writers Circle.

HO CHING YEE has been an avid reader and writer since primary school and hopes to continue writing as long as she is able to. She graduated from the National University of Singapore with a Bachelors Degree in English Literature (with Honours). She is also a History and Literature buff.

KATHY HOA has a passion for writing. She has never published any of her work but hopes to gain exposure by entering this competition. She is a university student in Canada, studying a helping profession. She writes a lot in her spare time and enjoys reading different novels on societal issues. She also enjoys watching films in the drama and sci-fi genre.

CARRIE HOOPER was born and raised in Elmira, New York. She received a Bachelor's degree in music performance from Mansfield University and Master's degrees in German and vocal performance from the State University of New York at Buffalo. She studied one year at the Royal University College of Music in Stockholm, Sweden as a Fulbright Scholar. Carrie taught German, Italian, and Romanian between 2002 and 2019 at Elmira College (Elmira, New York). She teaches voice and piano lessons, sings in a local chorus, gives vocal concerts, and plays the piano and organ at a church. She has published two collections of poetry and has translated a book, articles, and short stories from Albanian and Romanian into English.

JOSHUA IP is a poet, editor, and literary organiser. He has published four poetry collections with Math Paper Press, won the Singapore Literature Prize for his debut, *sonnets from the singlish*, and placed in three different categories of the Golden Point Award. He has edited nine literary anthologies, including the *A Luxury We Cannot Afford* and SingPoWriMo series. He directs Sing Lit Station, an overactive literary charity that runs community initiatives including SingPoWriMo, The Hawker Prize, and poetry.sg. He received the Young Artist Award from the National Arts Council (Singapore) in 2017. He is a PhD candidate at RMIT in the School of Media and Communications.

KATHY JIANG was born in Neijiang, China, and grew up in the suburbs of Washington, D.C. She is a recent graduate of the College of William and Mary, where she was the Editor-in-Chief of the *William and Mary Review*.

SADIE KAYE is a writer, presenter and producer. She presents quirky little podcasts, cheeky docs and comic slots for RTHK Radio 3 as RTHK's 'Miss Adventure' 香港電台冒險小姐 and herself. She can currently be heard presenting 'Mental Ideas', a weekly strand of Radio 3's '123 Show'. Her latest humorous audio column, 'Sharp Pains', starts broadcasting on RTHK Sept 29, 2020. Prior to returning to Hong Kong, where she started her career as a children's TV presenter on TVB, Sadie worked as a writer, a presenter, a filmmaker and a comic performer for TV broadcasters and production companies in London. In 2014 she wrote the humorous children's story 'The Wishing Machine'.

'War of Voices' is her first poem and she is tickled pink, purple, orange and yellow it has been awarded a place in Proverse Publishing's 2020 anthology. Her late grandfather, a poet, who also dabbled in banking, would be proud! She'd love to say he was an inspiration, but since his legacy is all in Welsh (and it's a sin to translate Welsh poetry into English, according to her mother) she can't *really* tell if he's been much of an influence or not. (Also, it's a sin to translate English poetry into Welsh, according to her father.)

R. J. KEELER was born in St. Paul, Minnesota, and grew up in the jungles of Colombia. He holds a BS in Mathematics from North Carolina State University, an MS in Computer Science from the University of North Carolina-Chapel Hill, an MBA from the University of California at Los Angeles, and a Certificate in Poetry from the University of Washington. An Honorman in the U.S. Naval Submarine School, he was Submarine Service (SS) qualified. He is a recipient of the Vietnam Service Medal, Honorable Discharge, and a Whiting Foundation Experimental Grant. He is a member of IEEE (technological society), AAAS (scientific society), and the Academy of American Poets. A former Boeing engineer.

My first poetry collection, *Detonation*, has just been published by Wipf and Stock.

LYNDA MCKINNEY LAMBERT lives in western Pennsylvania, USA. She is a retired professor of fine art and humanities, Geneva College, Beaver Falls, PA. Since retirement from her teaching schedule, she can devote her time every day to writing poetry and non-fiction essays. She has four published books available on Amazon at this time. Her themes are nature, seasons, passage of time,

Pilgrimage, and she is inspired by literature, music, and dance. Lynda writes spare poems and thoughtful personal essays. She writes, "I love nature, the heavenlies, walking my dogs, taking care of feral cats, standing in a meadow on a windy day with wildflowers all around me, and watching the sky in the middle of the night in winter.
Poetry is life. I fell in love with poetry as an undergraduate fine arts major. From the beginning, I was hooked. It's a wonder-filled life."

Dr HO-CHEUNG (PETER) LEE is the founding editor of BALLOONS Lit. Journal and author of the poetry chapbook *Something Celebrative or Immortal Under Another Birdless Sky* (Jamii Publishing). He was awarded Champion in both the Oxford Primary English Writing Competition (2019) and 'Love Is All Around' The 2nd Hong Kong Chinese & English Essay-Writing Competition (2019). His work (poetry/short stories/photography) has appeared in *Rattle*, **82 Review*, *Shearsman Magazine*, *Interpreter's House*, *The Writing Disorder*, *The Oddville Press*, and elsewhere. His poetry was shortlisted in Oxford Brookes University's International Poetry Competition (2016), for erbacce-prize for poetry (2017), twice for The Proverse Poetry Prize (2017 & 2018) and was a finalist of the Real Good Poem Prize (2019). He teaches English in Hong Kong.

J.P. LINSTROTH lives in the United States and has been writing poetry since he was a boy. He obtained a D.Phil. in Social and Cultural Anthropology from the University of Oxford and is an Adjunct Professor at Barry University and Faculty Member at the Catholic University of New Spain (UCNE). His books include: *Marching Against Gender Practice: Political Imaginings in the Basqueland* (2015, Lexington Books), *The Forgotten Shore* (Poetic Matrix Press, 2017), and *Epochal Reckonings* (Proverse Hong Kong, 2020, Winner of the 2019 Proverse Prize). Linstroth was a signatory of the Brussels Declaration for Peace to end ETA violence (2010). He was a co-recipient of an Alexander von Humboldt Foundation Grant (2005-2007) to study immigrant populations: Cubans, Haitians, and Guatemalan-Mayan immigrants in South Florida. He was awarded a J. William Fulbright Foreign Scholar Grant (2008-2009) to study urban Amerindians in Manaus, Brazil and to be a Visiting Professor at the Universida de Federal do Amazonas (UFAM). In 2017, he was awarded a Presidential Lifetime Achievement Award. Linstroth is a member of the Board of Directors of the International Peace Research Association Foundation (IPRAF). In 2019, he received a medal as a Gentleman of Merit and was inducted into La Noble Compañia de Bernardo de Gálvez (The Noble Order of Bernardo de Galvez). In addition to many academic articles, he writes opinion editorials (Op-

Eds) in many newspapers and online news sources, including *CounterPunch, Des Moine Register, Euroscientist, L.A. Progressive, PeaceVoice, The Houston Chronicle*, and *Londonderry Sentinel*. His academic research interests are cognition, ethno-nationalism, gender, genocide, history, immigrant advocacy, indigeneity, indigenous politics, indigenous rights, love, memory, minority rights, peace, peace-building, racism, social justice, and trauma.

IRIS LITT's newest book of poems is *Snowbird* from Finishing Line Press. Previous books are *What I Wanted to Say* from Shivastan Press, and *Word Love* from Cosmic Trend Publications. A recent short story publication is, 'Pissed Off', in the *Saturday Evening Post* Fiction Contest Anthology. She has had short stories, poems and articles in *Saturday Evening Post, Travelers' Tales, Confrontation, The Widow's Handbook, The London Magazine, the new renaissance, Earth's Daughters, Rambunctious Review* and many others. Awards include the Atlantic Monthly Award for College Writing, first prize in The Virtual Press short story contest, French Bread poetry award from Pacific Coast Journal. She was a finalist in the Valiant Literature 2020 Chapbook Contest. She has taught creative writing as an adjunct at SUNY/Ulster, Bard College, Arts Society of Kingston, Writers in the Mountains, New York Public Library and many other venues in New York City and the Hudson Valley. She lives in Woodstock, NY and winters on Anna Maria Island in Florida, which was the inspiration for 'Snowbird'.

S. E. LUDAN As an American Foreign Service Officer, S. E. Ludan has lived and worked in many different countries. S. E. Ludan began writing poetry several years ago, and would now like to publish.

K B RYAN JOSHUA MAHINDAPALA was born in 1991 in Singapore and graduated from the University of Liverpool with a bachelor's degree in Law in 2016. He was admitted to the Singapore Bar in 2020. He is a published writer of fiction, non-fiction and poetry. His work is an expression of his thoughts, feelings and opinions on current affairs, globalisation and history. He is an entrepreneur and the Founder/ Editor of Thinking Movement, a Medium publication centred around the formulation of strategic solutions in the areas of sustainability, social justice, inclusion, mental health and self-help with an Asian perspective. Ryan is an advocate for the promotion of arts, culture and sport. He is actively involved in numerous not-for-profit organisations where he provides his expertise in the area of social outreach, governance, law and strategy formulation. He is a management committee member of the Peranakan Indian Association of Singapore and a member of the Technical Committee of the Triathlon Association of Singapore where he is their social media lead strategist. Currently, Ryan is pursuing his postgraduate studies in Business Administration at the University of Strathclyde, United Kingdom. His work has been published on the Strathclyde Business School Blog, StrathUnion and the Strathclyde Telegraph. He draws inspiration from the people around him, his environment, past experiences, political figures and extensive travels around the world.

CARMINA MASOLIVER is a poet from south London, and founder of She Grrrowls feminist arts nights. She has been sharing her poetry on both the page and the stage for over a decade, and her small chapbook was published by Nasty Little Press in 2014, and her latest book, *Circles*, an illustrated epic poem, is published by Burning Eye Books (2019).

She published the *She Grrrowls* anthology with Burning Eye Books in 2017, which was named in the top 100 poetry books of that year by the Poetry School. She took She Grrrowls to the Edinburgh Fringe Festival between 2017-2019, and in 2018 she showcased a segment at the Women of the World Festival, at Southbank, London, UK. She toured with She Grrrowls in 2017 and 2020 thanks to Arts Council England (ACE) funding.

Carmina was long-listed for the Young Poet Laureate for London award in 2013, and the inaugural Jerwood Compton Poetry Fellowships in 2017. Most recently, she was longlisted for the Out-Spoken Prize in Performance Poetry 2018. An alumna of the Roundhouse Poetry Collective, she has featured at nights such as Bang Said the Gun, and festivals including Latitude, Bestival and Lovebox, both as a collective and individually. She has performed internationally whilst living abroad, in Singapore, and in Spain.

Whether creating stories through characters, making the political personal, or asserting that confessional poetry is cool, Carmina's aim is to connect with audiences, bringing them into her world, where she hopes they will find a bit of themselves. Her poetry is said to be formed of delicate constructions, quirky sense of humour and startling honesty.

WAYNE PAUL MATTINGLY is a multi-award-winning playwright whose work has been staged in NYC; Westchester & Putnam Counties, N.Y; Los Angeles, San Francisco; Bangor, Maine; Denton & Houston, Texas; Chamblee, GA; Valdez, Alaska; Kauai, Hawaii; and London, England.

Winner of the Tennessee Chapbook Prize; Arts & Letters Prize in Drama, Finalist, Milledgeville, GA; Denton Community Theatre, Method and Madness Competition & Festival, Third Prize, Denton,

TX; The Last Frontier Theatre Conference,/Susan Nims Distinguished Play Playwright Award Finalist, Valdez, Alaska; Phoenix Theatre, Hormel New Play Festival Finalist; The Ashland New Plays Festival Semi-finalist, Ashland, OR; Ronald Duncan Literary Prize Finalist, United Kingdom; 25th Annual International Playwriting Festival, Snapshot Production, Warehouse Theatre Co., London, U.K. and an IATC Cimientos Play Development Program Finalist, NYC.

He is a proud recipient of the 2020 BRIO Award; 2014 Helene Wurlitzer Foundation Fellowship Artists Residency Grant, Taos, NM; & to be a Grant Recipient of the 2014 & 2015 Disquiet International Literary Programs (short plays) in Lisbon, Portugal; and a 2015/16 & 2017/18 Can Serrat International Artists Residency Grant Recipient, in Barcelona, Spain.

He was a founding member & Dramaturg of The Misfits Ensemble, L.A.: Founding Artistic Director, Tiger's Heart Players, N.Y: a Dramatist Guild, & AEA member. Last stage appearance: 2013 Midtown International Theatre Festival, NYC, nominated for a Best Lead Actor Award. He has also directed dozens of works in both CA & NY. His latest full-length drama, *Anthem*, received reads with The Village Playwrights, NYC & Axial Theatre, Ossining, NY.

His work has appeared in the following publications: 2020, *Mingled Voices 4*; 2020 Best 10-Minute Plays; 2014 Best Women's Monologues; 1999 Best Women's Monologues & Best Stage Scenes, Smith & Kraus. More 10-Minute Plays for Teens, 2015, Applause Theatre & Cinema Books: and 2007 Poetry & Plays 14. Limited work is available at National New Play Network: nnpn.org.

JACK MAYER is a Vermont writer and pediatrician. His was the first pediatric practice in Eastern Franklin County, on the Canadian border, where he began writing essays, poems and short stories about his practice and hiking Vermont's Long Trail. He was a country doctor for ten years, often bartering medical care for eggs, firewood, and knitted afghans. From 1987 to 1991 Dr Mayer was a National Cancer Institute Fellow at Columbia University researching the molecular biology of cancer. Dr Mayer established Rainbow Pediatrics in Middlebury, Vermont in 1991 where he continues to practice primary care pediatrics. He is an Instructor in Pediatrics at the University of Vermont School of Medicine and an adjunct faculty for pre-medical students at Middlebury College. He was a participant at the Bread Loaf Writers' Conference in 2003 and 2005 (fiction) and 2008 (poetry). His first non-fiction book is *Life In A Jar: The Irena Sendler Project*. His new book, *Before The Court Of Heaven*, is historical fiction about the rise of Nazism, and has received 14 book awards. His collection of poems inspired and composed in wilderness, *Poems From The*

Wilderness, was published in Nov. 2020 and won the International Proverse Prize 2019."

MAYA MITOVA was born in the town of Blagoevgrad, Bulgaria and now lives in the town of Kresna in the neighbourhood of Blagoevgrad. She. graduated in Preschool education in 1990, and in Bulgarian philology in Blagoevgrad-Southwestern University in 1994. From 1994 up to the present she has worked as a teacher of Bulgarian Language and Literature in the "Father Paisii" Kresna, secondary school. She has published three anthologies, *Wanderlust* (2003) and *A romantic Sax for Summer Passers-By* (2017), and *Fireflies from the gardens of the Hesperides* (2020) .

She has won many poetry awards from national and international literary competitions, for example as follows.

In the sixth national competition for the most original character in a story or a poem by a modern Bulgarian author, "Irrelevant 2012", she was named, "Golden Irrelevant".

In the "Dora Gabe 2012" national award for young poets, she was awarded 1st prize by the Bulgarian Union of Writers, General Toshevo district.

She was named, "Albatros" for poetry, in Biela 2013 MONTENEGRO, awarded by the Literary Society, "Milutin Alempievich", of Frankfurt am Main in Germany.

In 2015, she won first prize in the XVI International Festival Melnik Poetry Evenings and also in the XV National Poetry Competition "Love ...".

She was Laureate of the III International Festival of Arts, "Morning Star", held in Bansko, Bulgaria, 2010.

Her poems have been translated into Serbian, Croatian, Macedonian, Romanian, English and German.

NATALIE NERA is a pen name of Natalie Dunn. She is a Czech writer, an author of two published novels as well as an editor of a poetry anthology in her mother tongue, who spent fifteen years in the UK with her British husband and children but has recently relocated to Prague. She writes in Czech, English and occasionally translates. Her written work has appeared in Czech, Russian, German, English, Bengali, Spanish and Romanian. Her work has appeared, for example, in *Mslexia, Eunoia Review, The Selkie, Litero Mania* and *Tvar*. She is Prose Editor and Co-Founder of *Fragmented Voices*, a small independent press based in Newcastle-upon-Tyne, United Kingdom, and Prague, Czech Republic. In January 2021, Natalie became a member of the Czech Centre of the International Pen Club.

HELEN OLIVER is an ESL teacher, materials writer and editor. She taught at the British Council in Hong Kong from 1978 – 1980, then lived and taught in Japan for 15 years, before returning to work in New Zealand. Working part-time now means she has more time for tai chi, music, books and poetry, family and friends. She loves the sea, kayaking and wandering the beaches of the Coromandel. Writing is becoming a passion. Having a poem published in *Mingled Voices 4: International Proverse Poetry Prize Anthology 2019* was her first international achievement.

RENA ONG is an English lady, married with one son, and lives in Singapore. There are many parks that she loves to wander around and she is delighted that her home is near the Singapore Botanical and Heritage Gardens, where one finds works of art and snippets of history amongst the beautiful landscapes, the   historical and contemporary meeting in harmony.

JUN (JANICE) PAN is an interpreter, researcher, and interpreter trainer. With a passion for reading and writing, she founded a Chinese poetry club and published a couple of Chinese poems (shi and ci) at the age of twelve at her birthplace in Xiangtan, Hunan. She then studied English language and literature in Jiangsu, and then, interpreting in Shanghai. She came to Hong Kong in 2008 for her PhD in interpreting studies and has been teaching interpreting and translation at local tertiary institutions since then.

Jun has worked as an interpreter (and translator) for many years, although her childhood dream was to become a writer, film director or painter. She found her childhood immersion in Chinese classic literature and culture important and invaluable in her life and career. Apart from introducing Chinese culture to many of her clients when she worked as an interpreter, Jun also participated in the translation of several classic works from English to Chinese, including John Ruskin's five-volumed *Modern Painters*, Lyman Frank Baum's *The Wonderful Wizard of Oz* and *The Marvelous Land of Oz*, etc.

Jun is now Associate Professor in the Department of Translation, Interpreting and Intercultural Studies at Hong Kong Baptist University, and was recently a visiting Faculty member at the State University of New York – Binghamton.

JOANNA RADWANSKA-WILLIAMS was born in Warsaw, Poland, and spent a part of her childhood in London, England. She received her B.A. with a double major in English and Linguistics (awarded with Highest Honors) and her Ph.D. in Linguistics from the University of North Carolina at Chapel Hill. Her dissertation was published as *A Paradigm Lost: The Linguistic Theory of Miko'aj Kruszewski* (Amsterdam: John Benjamins, 1993). She taught Slavic Linguistics (Polish and Russian) at the State University of New York at Stony Brook (1989-1994) and the University of Illinois at Chicago (1994-1995), and English Linguistics at Nanjing University (1996-1999) and the Chinese University of Hong Kong (1999-2003). In 2003, she joined Macao Polytechnic Institute, where she is now a full professor at the MPI-Bell Centre of English.

Joanna's poetry has been anthologized in several collections, including *Lingua Franca: An Anthology of Poetry by Linguists* (edited by Donna Jo Napoli and Emily Norwood Rando; Lake Bluff, Illinois: Jupiter Press, 1989), *Montage of Life* (Owings Mills, Maryland: The National Library of Poetry, 1998), *I Roll the Dice: Contemporary Macao Poetry* (edited by Christopher Kit Kelen and Agnes Vong; Macao: Association of Stories in Macao, 2008), *Lotus Field 2018: Reflections* (edited by Zi-yu Lin, Joanna Radwa'ska-Williams and Yunfeng Zhang; Macao: Macao Polytechnic Institute, 2018), *Mingled Voices 2: International Proverse Poetry Prize Anthology 2017*, *Mingled Voices 3: International Proverse Poetry Prize Anthology 2018*, *Mingled Voices 4: International Proverse Poetry Prize Anthology 2019* (edited by Gillian Bickley and Verner Bickley; Hong Kong: Proverse Hong Kong, 2018, 2019, 2020), and *Songs for Salamanders* (edited by Cat Dossett; Boston: Pen & Anvil Press, 2020).

C.N. RAJALAKSHMI (RAJI) is a poet and Language Teacher living in Hong Kong with her family. Her facebook page, "Raji's Poetic World", attracts an international audience. Raji's poetry explores culture and nature with deep underlying philosophies, inspired by human nature, religion and natural sceneries. For her, "Poetry is an artistic expression of the self". Her poems have appeared in various international anthologies and online platforms and she has read her work on RTHK.

COLIN RAMPTON is a retired teacher from England. He spent nearly 30 years working in Hong Kong. He has three children and five grandchildren and a long suffering wife (Hilary). He now lives in Hereford (UK) and enjoys travelling, writing and spending time with his family.

Decades ago, autodidact/ bloody-minded optimist KERRY RAWLINSON gravitated from sunny Zambian skies to solid Canadian soil. Now she stalks Literature & Art's Muses around the Okanagan Valley, still barefoot, her patient husband ensuring she's fed. Recent achievements: Edinburgh International FlashFiction Award; FishPoetryPrize; BestCanadianPoetry 2019 'Notable Poem.' Newer acceptances: ArcPoetry, Banshee Literary, Synchronized Chaos; Foreign Literary, AcrossTheMargin, Painted Bride, TupeloQuarterly, ConnecticutRiverReview, Pedestal.

M. ANN REED is a researcher, poet, Chinese calligrapher-brush painter and professor of English Literature and Theory of Knowledge. She has taught in Malaysia, Ukraine, Bosnia-Herzegovina and China where traditional cultures regard literature a medical art. Her postdoctoral research studies the mending arts of English poetry and drama. Her Chinese calligraphy and brush paintings have been exhibited in Portland, Oregon and at the Shenzhen Fine Arts Museum in China. Her poems have been published in various literary journals. Her chapbook, *making oxygen, remaining inside this pure hollow note*, has been recently released by Finishing Line Press.

VINNI C RELWANI lives in Singapore, calling it home for the last 20 years, with a soft-spot for Hong Kong where she was born and raised. A homemaker and mum, Vinni enjoys writing, and is in her zone when writing poetry and short stories.

ANGELO RIZZI was born in 1956, in Sant' Angelo Lodigiano, Italy. His mother tongue is Italian, but he is a polyglot poet, writing in Arabic, Spanish, Italian and French. He has a degree in Arabic Language, Culture and Literature from Bordeaux University, France and a degree in Italian Language, Culture and Literature from Nice University, France.

In 2006, he attended the UNESCO Congress, "Dialogue among the Nations".

He has received about fifty literary awards, including, in 2004, the prestigious Nosside World Prize and, in 2019, the first Award for poetry in a foreign language at Città di Voghera, Italy.

He has participated in international poetry meetings and recitals in Rome, Italy; Havana, Cuba; Brazil; India; Paris, Breil-sur-Roya, and Mouans-Sartoux, France; Monaco; Curtea de Argeş, Romanía; and Djerba, Tunisia.

In 2015, the ® Academia Internacional de Ciéncias, Létras and Art ALPAS XXI in Cruz Alta (Porto Alegre), R/S Brazil, nominated him International Correspondent Academic.

Rizzi is a member of REMES (Red Mundial de Escritores en Español); World Poets Society; Poetas del Mundo and SELAE (Sociedad de Escritores Latino-Americanos y Europeos).

He collaborated with the multi-language magazine, *A Oriente* (Milan, Italy 2000, 2001), and the magazine *Umbral* (Santa Clara, Cuba, 2005).

He has published 20 collections of poems and poetic prose. His poems have appeared in anthologies and magazines in Italy, the United States, Switzerland, Cuba, Argentina, Kuwait, Spain, Brazil, Romania, Hong Kong, India, Bolivia and soon in Kenya.

HALIL SUAT SARAÇ is a scholar of things: matters, ideas, words and worlds.

JOSE MANUEL SEVILLA was born in Barcelona in 1959 and has been living in Hong Kong since 2003.

His published poetry books (in Spanish) are: *From the limits of paradise* (1991), *Alice in Ikea's Catalogue*, *The Night of Europe* (2004), *Ashes of Auschwitz and Eighteen Dogs* (awarded the Angel Urrutia award in 2009), and *Family Album* (2016).
His English-language poetry collection, *The Year of the Apparitions*, was published in 2020.

His plays for the theatre are: "El Puente" / "The Bridge" (written after a trip to Croatia during the last European war, and staged in Catalonia, Spain (2000) and Hong Kong (2011), "Sombras, Sol y Flamenco" (Ballet by Ingrid Sera-Gilet, Hong Kong), 2012 and "Kennedy" 2016.

His poem, 'Sonia Wants to Rent an Apartment' won first prize in the Asian Cha Poetry Contest, "Encountering", in 2012 . His group of poems, "Of Words and Keys" was included in the Proverse Prize 2017 anthology *Mingled Voices 2*, his poem, 'Voice and Verse', the *Asian Cha* Tenth Anniversary Anthology (2018) and his poem, 'The Talking Photo' in *Mingled Voices 3* (2019).

His work has also appeared in Spanish-language anthologies, *Trayecto contiguo* (1993) and *Otro Canto* (2013).

ALLEGRA JOSTAD SILBERSTEIN grew up on a farm in Wisconsin but has lived in California since 1963. Her love of poetry began as a child when her mother would recite poems as she worked. Now that she is retired there is more time for singing and dancing as well as poetry. She has three chapbooks of poetry. In the spring of 2015, Cold River Press published her first book and she is widely published in journals such as *Blue Unicorn, California Quarterly, Iodine Poetry* and *Poetry*

Now. In March of 2010 she was honored to become the first Poet Laureate for the city of Davis, CA.

WESLEY D. SIMS has published three chapbooks of poetry: When Night Comes, Finishing Line Press, Georgetown, Kentucky, 2013; Taste of Change, Iris Press, Oak Ridge, TN, 2019; and A Pocketful of Little Poems, Amazon, 2020. His work has appeared in *Artemis Journal*, *Bewildering Stories*, *Connecticut Review*, *G.W. Review*, *Liquid Imagination*, *Pine Mountain Sand and Gravel*, *Plum Tree Tavern*, *Novelty Magazine*, *Poem*, *Poetry Quarterly*, *Time of Singing*, *The South Carolina Review*, and several others.

HAYLEY ANN SOLOMON is an author, librarian and poet. She has been particularly fortunate during the course of her writing career and has thoroughly enjoyed her excursions into multiple genres – fiction fantasy, literary short stories, poetry, historical romance and even the odd non-fiction academic article. She is very grateful to Proverse Hong Kong, who has recognised her several times in the past, in particular the 2017 and 2018 Supplementary Prizes in the annual Proverse Prize. Poetry is one of Hayley's particular interests – she enjoys the vehicle for succinct delivery of philosophy, sonic beauty and metric rhythms.

Her Poetry collection, *Celestial Promise* (Proverse 2017) – available through Amazon and the Chinese University of Hong Kong Press, Hong Kong – encapsulates her view of the beauty of poetry as a medium for expression – the variability of mood, meter, rhythm, theme, philosophy, high jinx and emotional resonance in juxtaposition or synergy, perhaps, with the constraints of form.

Hayley is the mother of a lawyer, a scientist and a software engineer. She is the wife of a surgeon and is, in her spare time, a classical soprano. She is studying for her ATCL in music and sings with the Marlborough Singers, so her life is a rather eclectic potpourri of different thoughts, viewpoints and momentum!

ROBIN SUSANTO was born in Indonesia. After many departures and arrivals he found his way to this Coast Salish territory, a.k.a. Vancouver, Canada, where he continues to immigrate homeward. His work has appeared in various publications, and has won prizes and mentions including in the W. H. Henry Drummond contest, the Ross & Davis Mitchell Canada 150 Contest for Faith and Writing, and the A3 Review.

LUISA TERNAU was born and raised in Trieste, Northeastern Italy. After graduating at the University of Trieste she moved to the UK (London and one year in Wales). She obtained an MA in English Literature at King's College, University of London. Since then Luisa has lived in a number of countries across three continents. She has been based in Hong Kong for the last ten years. Luisa likes to write poems and short stories. Her inspiration is life in its multiple facets. She is interested in literature, ranging from poetry to folk tales, from all over the world and from every era. Luisa won a third prize in the inaugural Proverse Poetry Prize competition and her poems have appeared in each of the Proverse Poetry Prize *Mingled Voices* Anthologies.

EDWARD A. TIESSE recently returned to Washington State after living for several years in the Chicago area. From his home on clear days, he can see Mount Baker and the Canadian Cascades. Living so close to Canada makes it easy to slip across the border when it becomes necessary.

Edward A. Tiesse has many interests. He loves to cook and recently began baking bread which he soon learned is much like writing poetry. That is, the combinations of flour, water and yeast have many variables and so baking is much like trying to find the right word and its place in a line. Edward's poetry has been published in *The Front Porch Review*, *The Sea Letter* and in the Proverse Poetry Prize Anthologies, *Mingled Voices*.

BIBIANA TSANG is an undergraduate student at the University of Hong Kong. One of her poems, 'Lines Written in Spring' is featured in *People, Pandemic & Protest – The KongPoWriMo 2020 Anthology*. As an amateur poet, her other interests include Chinese art history and Romantic poetry which often inspires her poetic works. In 2020, she has been awarded as the winner of the HKUMS Asian Art Essay Prize Competition. She is the founder of the blog Otiose Literatus, where she regularly shares knowledge on art and literature, and occasionally, her poems. She has always been passionate about encouraging those around her to appreciate the liberal arts and to create works of their own. The blog – Otiose Literatus is her "small but significant attempt to achieve this."

ROGER UREN is an Australian but he has spent over half his adult life in Asia. He has lived in Hong Kong for thirteen years, in Beijing for four years, as well as lengthy periods of time in Malaysia, India and Taiwan. He worked as an Australian diplomat and public servant from 1974 until 2001, and then served as Vice President of Phoenix Satellite Television in Hong Kong for twelve years. He speaks both Mandarin

Chinese and Bahasa Indonesian, which he used when he was working at the Australian High Commission in Kuala Lumpur. He has a long history of involvement with literature, and has written books on Chinese erotic art, on the life of the long-time chief of the Chinese Communist secret service, as well as a novel set in 1980s Beijing and a collection of poetry that he has written from the 1960s through to the 2000s. He notes that human society has many problems and one of the themes of his recent poetry is how mankind needs to connect different societies and counter the way that egomania tends to influence many global leaders.

ROD USHER is an Australian poet and novelist living in Extremadura, Spain. He has published three poetry collections, most recently *Convent Mermaid* (IP, Brisbane), and three novels, most recently *Poor Man's Wealth* (HarperCollins). His poems have appeared in many literary magazines and anthologies, including *Best Australian Poems 2015* and *Best Australian Love Poems*. He is a former senior writer and editor for TIME magazine in Europe.

PETER COE VERBICA grew up on a commercial cattle ranch in Northern California. He obtained a BA and JD from Santa Clara University and an MS from the Massachusetts Institute of Technology. He is married and has four daughters.

SARAH VETTER was born in and raised in rural Canada, just outside of the nation's capital city, Ottawa. Writing and reading are passions she's never been without, the cost of which being that she's often unable to differentiate between her own experiences and stories she's read.
Currently, Vetter lives in Shanghai and has easily taken to an urban, metropolitan lifestyle.

RENEE WADE lives in Mangawhai, a small rural town in New Zealand. She is a primary school teacher and English literature is her favourite subject to teach. She is honoured and finds it a privilege to use and learn Te Reo Maori; she encourages her students to use Te Reo as it is, "a beautiful language to learn in our rich and diverse culture."
Renee writes poems as a way to let go of stress and it promotes a positive well-being for her. Many of her poems are inspired by Mary Shelly and she adores the eighteenth century era. At times she can write with the pen flowing from her spirit, other she is blank. "I believe writing to be a very spiritual process for me and being enlightened to write can happen in the strangest of places and times. Some of my

poems are free flow and some are to promote English language features. Writing is definitely a hobby of mine."

VICTORIA WALVIS was born in London and lives in Hong Kong where she teaches English. She is an enthusiastic member of the Peel Street Poets, and organises weekly free creative writing workshops for adults. She was longlisted for the National Poetry Competition in 2019 and shortlisted for The York Poetry Prize in 2020. She is currently working on her first collection of poems.

ANSON HONGHUA WANG, PhD, is an Assistant Professor in Translation. Her research interests are interpreter and translator training, gender and translation and second language acquisition. She is a practicing translator and interpreter. Besides research, she has a wide range of interests including reading, watching movies and hiking. She has been serving as Executive Committee Member of the Hong Kong Association of University Women since 2013. She is also a member of the International Association for Translation and Intercultural Studies.

BRUCE ARLEN WASSERMAN, DDS, MFA, assembled his first poetry manuscript at the age of seventeen and later farmed and worked as a blacksmith in his twenties and as an editor before and through his first graduate degree program. In 2016, he was nominated for a Pushcart Prize and his short story was a semi-finalist for the 2017 Francine Ringold Awards for New Writers. He won the 2019 Anna Davidson Rosenberg Award, second place.

He received an MFA from Vermont College of Fine Arts in 2017. His writing has been published in the *Proverse Poetry Prize Anthology*, *The Fredericksburg Literary and Art Review*, *The River Heron Review*, *Kindred Literary Magazine* and *Broad River Review*. He is a literary critic for the *New York Journal of Books* and the *Washington Independent Review of Books* and a Graduate Assistant at the MFA in Writing program of VCFA. His fiction manuscript, The Aroma of Light, was a finalist with LSU Press and is currently represented by Mark Gottlieb of Trident Media Group. Bruce creates visual art as a potter (BruceArlenWassermanStudio.com) where he draws from the reservoir of poetry and his experience in working iron and wood, correlating a continued exploration of language, function and esoteric form. At other times he performs as a musician in a band, trains horses on occasion and is a dentist in clinical practice.

GEORGE WATT has held teaching, research and administrative positions at universities in Australia, USA, Japan and Macau. He took up the writing of poetry late in life, graduating in creative writing from the University of Edinburgh in Scotland. His first full-length collection of poetry, *Sandpaper Swimming*, has recently been published by Flying Island Books.

MOCCO WOLLERT was born in Germany of French heritage (her maiden name is still French). Mocco survived not only the bombings of her home town Cologne but also the horrific destruction of Dresden, in World War II.

From an early age she escaped into writing about her feelings, desires and fantasies. Her love of French literature and French poets resulted in her spending quite some time in Paris.

She migrated to Australia in 1958, following a man she loved unconditionally and to whom she was married till he passed away in 2018. Her "school English" was a great handicap but, as an avid reader, she learned quickly and her first poem in English was published in 1967.

Mocco writes from her heart, her poetry is honest and understandable, people can identify with her words. Her European background gave her the freedom to express herself without the restrictions of English convention. Love is a theme that runs through most of her work .

Like many writers, Mocco has varied sides to her writing and in her previous books she explores 'inspirational Words' as well as the stark and dark times of the war in a disturbing and serious anthology, published in 1988.

Mocco lives in Queensland, Australia. Her life is dedicated to writing.

ELIZABETH (LIBBY) WONG, CBE ISO JP
Elizabeth Wong, popularly known as, "Libby", studied English at the University of Hong Kong, under the tutelage of Professor Edmund Charles Blunden, then Head of the English Department and British Poet Laureate. She graduated with a B.A. Hons. Degree, followed by a post-graduate diploma with distinction in Education. She also attended sponsored courses in New Zealand and at the Harvard Business School, USA, respectively.

A registered teacher in Hong Kong, she taught English before pursuing a career in the Administrative Service of the Hong Kong Government, serving in various key positions, including the following.

In the early 1980s, as Music Administrator, she promoted music and the performing arts and was instrumental in setting up the Academy for the Performing Arts (APA) in Hong Kong.

In 1987, as Director of the Social Welfare Department, she introduced major reforms, including the introduction of the Senior Citizens Card.

In 1990, she was appointed Secretary for Health and Welfare and was responsible for setting up the Hospital Authority (HA) in Hong Kong.

In 1995, she took early retirement from the civil service to go into politics. She was elected with the highest number of votes to Hong Kong's last Legislative Council under British rule in 1995.

In 1997, she quit politics to write. She has published novels, plays, poems and short stories. She has also worked with Hong Kong students on drama, poetry and creative writing.

She was a columnist with *Ming Pao* ('English with Celebrity') and *The South China Morning Post* ('On Second Thought').

For her services to Hong Kong, Her Majesty Queen Elizabeth II awarded her an Imperial Service Order in 1989 and appointed her a CBE in 1994. In 1995, she was made a JP and an Hon. Fellow of the Academy for the Performing Arts.

WAN-TING (JOYCE) WU is a digital creator and a poet based in California. She received her BA in English with an emphasis in Applied Language studies with a minor in TESL in just three years and has published two poetry collections on Wattpad: The Harry Styles Project and Fairytales. As a person who struggles daily depression, anxiety, PTSD, and many other chronic illnesses, she wants to use her poetry to empower her readers and help them find the strength to overcome their own demons. She also prides herself in having the ability to talk to and befriend any stranger, which, she says, "could surely be an introvert's worst nightmare."

THE EDITORS

GILLIAN BICKLEY, born and educated in the United Kingdom, has lived mostly in Hong Kong since 1970. She has been a member of the Society of Authors in the United Kingdom since her school days.

Her poetry collections include *For the Record and other Poems of Hong Kong, Moving House and other Poems from Hong Kong, Sightings: a collection of poetry, China Suite and other Poems, Perceptions*, and *Grandfather's Robin*. Selections from these collections have been published bilingually: in the English-Romanian *Poems/Poeme* (Romanian translation by Carolina Ilica and Dumitru M. Ion) and the English-Italian, *Avvistamenti, pensieri e sentimenti* (Italian translation by Luisa Ternau). Two collections – *Moving House* and *For the Record* – have also been published in Chinese; individual poems have been published in Arabic, Catalan, Chinese, Czech, French, German, Romanian, Turkish and other languages. *Over the Years* (2017) is a selection from her previously published work, selected by Verner Bickley. In 2014, she was awarded the "Grand Prix Orient-Occident Des Arts" at the 18th International Festival, "Curtea de Argeş Poetry Nights", held in Romania. Gillian Bickley is one of the Hong Kong poets discussed in Agnes S. L. Lam's study, *Becoming poets: The Asian English Experience*.

Gillian has written or edited several non-fiction books in different fields: *The Golden Needle: The Biography of Frederick Stewart, 1836-1889 (founder of Hong Kong Government Education)*, Hong Kong Baptist University and David C. Lam Institute for East-West Studies, 1997; *Hong Kong Invaded! A '97 Nightmare*, University of Hong Kong Press, Hong Kong, 2001; *The Development of Education in Hong Kong, 1841-1897: as revealed through the Early Education Reports of the Hong Kong Government, 1848-1896*, Proverse Hong Kong, Hong Kong, 2002; *The Stewarts of Bourtreebush*, Centre for Scottish Studies, University of Aberdeen, Scotland, 2003; *A Magistrate's Court in 19th Century Hong Kong: Court in Time*, Proverse Hong Kong, first edition, 2005; second edition, 2009; *The Complete Court Cases of Magistrate Frederick Stewart*, Proverse Hong Kong, 2008; *In Time of War* (in collaboration with Richard Collingwood-Selby), an edition based on the writings of Henry C.S. Collingwood-Selby (1898-1992), Lieutenant Commander in the Royal Navy, Proverse Hong Kong, 2013, *Through American Eyes: The Journals of George Washington (Farley) Heard (1837-1875)*, Proverse Hong Kong, 2017; *Journeys with a Mission: Travel Journals of The Right Revd George Smith (1815-1871), first Bishop of Victoria, Hong Kong (1849-1865)*, Proverse Hong Kong, 2018.

Five of these fourteen English-language books received publication support from Hong Kong Arts Development Council (HKADC) and four from the Lord Wilson Heritage Trust. The extensive research necessary for seven of the non-fiction works listed was made possible by research grants awarded by the Hong Kong Baptist University and one was supported by a private sponsor.

Dr Bickley was Senior Lecturer / Associate Professor in the Department of English at the Hong Kong Baptist University for twenty-two years. She has been a full-time faculty member at the University of Lagos, Nigeria; the University of Auckland, New Zealand; and at the University of Hong Kong.

For several years, Gillian was an adjudicator at the world-famous Hong Kong Schools Music & Speech Association's annual Speech Festival and has also been a judge for the Budding Poets' Society Hong Kong.

More recently, as co-ordinator of literary activities for the English-Speaking Union Hong Kong, a non-profit registered educational charity, she has led reading appreciation sessions which are open to the community and assists to deliver reading courses at local schools. She has worked with the Gifted Education Section of the Education Bureau to encourage creative writing among students. On a freelance basis, she has taught creative reading / writing courses at the Hong Kong Academy for Gifted Education (HKAGE) and at the University of Hong Kong School for Professional and Continuing Education (HKU SPACE) and been a guest lecturer on poetry at Lingnan University Community College. Her creative reading / writing course at HKU SPACE continues to be offered. In 2016, she managed twenty and hosted seventeen meet-the-author events at a Hong Kong bookshop. On occasion, she accepts invitations to speak at school Reading Festivals and similar.

Following her career in academia, Gillian has become an experienced publisher, project-manager, text editor, and production manager, including of poetry, non-fiction, fiction and academic writing. She has been President of the Hong Kong Association of University Women and has recently stepped aside from her role as Council Member and a Vice-President of the Royal Asiatic Society (Hong Kong).

THE EDITORS

VERNER BICKLEY was born in the North-West of England, and educated there, in Wales and London, and has lived in Asian and Pacific countries for over fifty years.

He has been scholar, teacher, manager, broadcaster, stage and film actor and cultural diplomat in a life often enlivened by music and song, dance and entertainment.

Verner's many scholarly articles and book publications are mainly on educational and cross-cultural topics. He has however also published two volumes of memoirs: *Footfalls Echo in the Memory* and *Steps To Paradise And Beyond*. His five-book graded poetry anthology, *Poems to Enjoy*, has been popular since the 1960s. These now benefit from accompanying recordings of all poems in the texts (read mostly by himself, but some by his wife, Gillian), as well as from teaching and performance notes. He is a member of the United Kingdom Society of Authors.

With his wife, Gillian, Verner Bickley is joint-publisher of Proverse Hong Kong and co-founder of the Proverse Prize and the Proverse Poetry Prize.

Verner was a naval officer in pre-independent Sri Lanka and India. He served in the Colonial Education Service in Singapore and, later, as a British Council officer in post-independence Burma, in Indonesia and Japan. In Hawaii from 1971 to 1981, he served as the Director and for a period Chairman of Directors of the Culture Learning Institute at the East-West Center, established by the US Congress in Hawaii in 1960 and functioning as a US-based institution for public diplomacy with international governance, staffing, students and Fellows.

From 1972 to 1980, Verner led a small team of anthropologists, cross-cultural psychologists and linguists, focusing on the different ways in which individuals and whole societies cope in bicultural and multicultural contexts and how they address problems presented by different cultural norms. Among many interesting projects, his Institute provided for the pioneering voyage of the canoe, *Hōkūle'a*, from Hawaii to Tahiti, disproving the theories of Thor Heyerdahl.

Verner was instrumental in bringing to conferences in Honolulu writers who included Guy Amirthanayagam, Leon Edel, Vincent Eri, Nissim Ezekial, Reuel Denney, Janet Frame, Allen Ginsberg, Syd Harrex, Thomas Keneally, Maxine Hong-Kingston, Arun Kolatkhar, Ananda Murthy, Kenzaburo Oe, Kushwant Singh, Kamala Markandaya, R.K. Narayan, A.K. Ramanajuan, E.R. Sarachchandra, Wole Soyinka and Albert Wendt.

After leaving Hawaii, and while in Saudia Arabia for a two-year assignment with the national airline, Saudia, Verner was responsible for a multi-national staff of 100 persons, mainly, but not exclusively, in Jeddah and Riyadh.

In 1983, Verner was appointed founding director of the Institute of Language in Education in Hong Kong and held that post until 1992. During that period, he created and led annual International conferences on Applied Linguistics and founded and directed the journal, the ILEJ.

Refusing to retire, Verner continues to live in Hong Kong where he writes and publishes on a variety of topics. He was founding Chairman of the English-Speaking Union (Hong Kong) and continued as Chairman of the Executive Committee for sixteen years. He recently passed this responsibility over to a new chairman, but in his capacity as Chairman Emeritus continues with his own portfolio of tasks. As Chairman, he traveled for many years to the Mainland of China to join other judges of the national Public-Speaking Competition organised by national media. He was an adjudicator for the Hong Kong Schools Music and Speech Association's annual Speech Festival for many years and for a while was Representative in Hong Kong for Trinity College London.

Verner Bickley's experiences have created in him an interest in cross-cultural experiences and attitudes and in a desire to communicate what he has learnt. Through his memoirs as well as his personal contacts, he hopes not only to interest others, but to encourage them to build on their own desire to learn about and empathise with other cultures.

PROVERSE HONG KONG

Together, Gillian and Verner Bickley are the publishers of Proverse Hong Kong, a Hong Kong-based press which publishes both local and international authors, including non-native users of English. They are also co-founders of two annual international literary prizes for work submitted in English: in 2008, they founded the Proverse Prize for unpublished book-length fiction, non-fiction or poetry, and, in 2016, they established the Proverse Poetry Prize (for single poems which may have been previously published in a language other than English). In the case of both prizes, entries are received from around the world.

Beginning in 2007 up to December 2020, Proverse has managed, edited and published about 129 English-language books by Hong Kong and international writers, five Chinese-language books, one English / Chinese and one English / Italian bilingual book. Of the English-language books, about twenty-two have been awarded publication support by Hong Kong Arts Development Council (HKADC), four by Lord Wilson Heritage Trust and two by the Ride Fund for publication in the Royal Asiatic Society Hong Kong Studies series. One received a publication grant from the Ministry of Culture of the Czech Republic and one received a publication grant from the Ministry of Culture and Tourism of the Republic of Turkey.

Twice a year, Proverse organises literary events in Hong Kong, open to the public. New books are launched, writers are introduced and launching authors give brief talks. Announcements are made relating to the current year's Proverse Prize for unpublished fiction, non-fiction or poetry, and the Proverse Poetry Prize (for single short poems); prizes are presented to those winning authors who are present. Videos of some of these events are available on Youtube and photos of most of them are available on the Proverse website, proversepublishing.com.

Gillian and Verner work hard to bring authors before the reading public and to encourage reading as well as writing. On three occasions, they have administered Reading Development Grants awarded by the Hong Kong Arts Development Council. In 2016, as implementation of one of these, they arranged twenty meet-the-author sessions, held at a Hong Kong bookshop. To reach an international audience, edited videos of these talks are available on Youtube.

Of the titles published by Proverse, several have attracted a Preface or advance appreciation from figures of international reputation, most notably perhaps, from Václav Havel (for the English translation of Olga Walló's *Tightrope: A Bohemian Tale*).

Two titles (Peter Gregoire's, *Article 109* and *The Devil You Know*) were best sellers at Dymocks Hong Kong.

The publication by Proverse of the late Sophronia Liu's book, *A Shimmering Sea*, was a major argument in the award to Sophronia of a posthumous PhD at the University of Minnesota.

Other writers published by Proverse have also benefited in their literary careers, a couple of them taking a leadership role in local literary groups.

Gillian's and Verner's own books and all those by other authors published by Proverse, are available internationally as well as locally, including through the Chinese University of Hong Kong Press. There are copies in the British Library and other legal deposit libraries in the United Kingdom, and in the Hong Kong Public Library system, as well as in many university and public libraries world-wide. Books by Australian writers have been deposited in the National Library of Australia and similar deposits are ongoing in other countries.

POETS' NOTES AND COMMENTARIES

[1] Vinita Agrawal says this of her poem, 'The Walk of Hunger.'
"In April 2020 millions of migrant labourers were displaced from their jobs. Because of the pandemic, a total lockdown was announced in India from March to May 2020. Businesses and factories shut down, restaurants closed and street vendors were left without work because everyone was confined to their homes. As a result most of the daily-wage working-class people who had come to cities for their livelihood were rendered almost penniless. They had no income and as a result they could not pay their rent. They were forced to give up their accommodation in the cities and return to their villages – where most of them had roots, a home and a field to grow their own food.

"But the journey back to their roots was not an easy one. As a result of the lockdown, there were no trains or buses to take them back to their villages. They had no option but to travel on foot. Most of the labourers belonged to the northern states of Uttar Pradesh and Bihar. This was a long distance away from the urban work centres of Delhi and Mumbai. Particularly Mumbai – a distance of almost 1200 kilometres. Almost an impossible trek in the scorching summer season. Still, these brave workers – both men and women along with their little children, undertook this daunting journey. Without money, without food or water, with only their will intact. Will and the intent to return to their roots from where there would be no threat of getting uprooted.

"They, along with their families, walked hundreds of miles to their respective villages. Hundreds perished on the way as the journey proved too arduous. Sunstroke, hunger and exhaustion overcame many of these vulnerable travellers. It was heart-rending to hear the news of young children perishing because of the difficult journey. Many writers and poets responded to the tragedy in the only way they could – through words.

"It was generally felt that a kinder attitude on the part of their employers, some compassion on behalf of their landlords and better transport arrangements by the government could have prevented these tragic deaths.

"I too responded to these tragic events by writing poems such as 'The Walk of Hunger'."

<u>Note from Vinita Agrawal</u>
Parle G Biscuits are a very popular brand of sustenance biscuits in India. If there's no money to buy proper food, there's always enough to pick up a packet of Parle G, as they are extremely affordable.

2 Joy Al-sofi wrote this about her poem, 'Sometimes A Poem Is'. "There is a saying, 'To a hammer, everything looks like a nail.' If language is a tool, then everything looks like it can be put into words. Language insists that we should try to.

"Language soon takes on a life of its own, leading us to mistake the words for the reality. Language moves in discrete form; words are reductive and digital: long and short, then and now, word and space, here and gone.

"Poetry is how we distill the essence of language.

"On one level I wanted explore three aspects of language: what language has done, is doing, and what it can't do. This poem explores the first two of these. The third – if not beyond words – is yet to come."

3 Of, 'Taking Liberties (With Random Pandemic Haiku-ish Hong Kong Thoughts) – 2020', Joy Al-sofi wrote, "2020 hasn't lent itself to clear vision or a sense of continuity. Rather we got smacked in the beginning of the year with the Covid-19 virus. Invisible things were happening and preparing unprecedented effects. And instead of facing this in unity, whether as a united species, or society, the human species have ended up with a deadly, disjointed, antagonistic and fragmented response, leaving us facing a very uncertain future.

"Additionally, by mid-year, we had a national security law. There has not been a moment of repose.

"This poem was a way of expressing some of what was dispiriting and disorienting up till the end of June from a variety of perspectives.

"It came out in haiku structure, but didn't adhere to traditional haiku rules for subject and non-poetical elements so it became haiku-ish. I tried to capture both the content of what was happening and the disconcerting aspects many of us were/are feeling."

4 Joy provides her original sources as below.

1. Su Shi (Translation https://www.poemhunter.com/su-shi/)
Sunset cloud gather far excess clear cold
Milky Way silent turn jade plate
This life this night not long good
Next year bright moon where see

2. Li Bai (Translation http://www.chinese-poems.com/lb11.html)
What place under heaven most hurts the heart?
Laolao Ting, for seeing visitors off.
The spring wind knows how bitter it is to part,

The willow twig will never again be green.

3. Wang Wei (Translation https://www.chinawhisper.com/top-10-most-influential-chinese-poems-in-history/)
All alone in a foreign land,
I am twice as homesick on this day
When brothers carry dogwood up the mountain,
Each of them a branch-and my branch missing

Of her poem, 'Thoughts On Three Chinese Poems', Joy Al-sofi wrote, "Most times, other people's poetry moves me to read more poetry. Or inspires me to write poems of my own, often on unrelated topics. But, for whatever reason, and this has been true over many years, Chinese poetry causes me to respond directly to the poems themselves and to write of that response in poems of my own.

"1. The first poem, by Su Shi AKA Su Dong Bo, evoked both a paraphrase of the first ideas set out in his poem, but with a twist in the final idea. My poem, as his, speaks of the impermanence of worldly possessions and high position that cause us to turn our backs on the natural world. The persona questions where he might be in the future when the moon again rises at the same time of year.

"I, too, wanted to show that the natural world, exemplified by the rising moon, will continue. But my poem asks a different question, not just that there would be changes and where the persona might be, but suggesting that the future will be less bright/fruitful than now.

"2. This poem by Li Bai poses questions which provoked a direct response to those questions. This persona considers feelings that some may have in our community, and reflects on whether there is any way to recover when what is fundamental seems to have been lost.

"3. This poem by Wang Wei caused me to write along a parallel path through the persona's ideas of loneliness, homesickness, and imagining the family back home celebrating a holiday without him. He envisions how his departure has left a deep chasm in the family, in their daily lives and thoughts, by focussing on the disruption of a holiday celebration. I turned to a well-known festival to show this. His family honors him by putting his lantern into the stream with their own. But, instead of a brightly-lit one, which would say that nothing had changed, instead, they send a dark one, creating a line with his place seemingly missing but actually there. The lantern being there says he is never far from their hearts and thoughts, but, being unseen, they have made visible the loss they feel and the empty space in their hearts that they have kept waiting for him."

[5] Shikha Bansal explains that, "The inspiration of 'Never Alone' came from experiencing some of the ill effects of the excessive use of social media. The poem was also a step back from the heavily socialized and networked lives we sometimes tend to lead in urban hubs, and the 'groupthink' that leaves us little room for our own thoughts, originality and creativity."

[6] Shikha Bansal writes that, "The inspiration of 'New City' came from the experience of moving to new countries as an expatriate. It is the first, overwhelming emotion you might feel at the newness of it all. From transplanting yourself to making the new city your home and thriving in it, is a long journey. This is a small snippet from that journey."

[7] <u>Note</u> on Alan Bern's poem, 'Rodin's *Ugolin* to Dante's *Ugolino*':
A statue by French artist, August Rodin, is named, "Ugolin et ses enfants". In his *Divine Comedy* (*Divina Commedia*), Italian poet, Dante Alighieri depicts Count Ugolino and his children. This poem reflects on these two artistic interpretations of one historical personality.
Alan Bern writes as follows:
"*Conte Ugolino*: Ugolino della Gherardesca, is one of the most memorable of Dante's characters in his *Commedia*.

"At the very bottom of Hell, *Inferno Cantos XXXII-XXXIII*, up to his neck in excruciating ice, he gnaws <u>forever</u> on the back-skull of Archbishop Ruggieri degli Ubaldini, a political enemy and the one who locked him in a tower along with two of Ugolino's sons and two of his grandsons. No wonder he gnaws on Ruggieri's skull!

"Although it may seem like revenge for Ugolino, this is only partially so: he is trapped in the ice with Ruggieri <u>forever</u>, and both participate, as a dreadful couple, in a most brutal Dantean *contrapasso*; that is, 'a process either resembling or contrasting with the sin itself.' (en.wikipedia.org/wiki/Contrapasso)

"So what is the sin and why does Ugolino capture our imaginations and remain in memory? I agree with many that the sin for both Ugolino and Ruggieri is a species of fraud, *political treachery*; and we are captured most by the possibility – both historical and an implication in the *Commedia* – that Ugolino cannibalized his sons (and grandsons) in order to survive – or perhaps to spare them the pain of starving to death? In either case, horrific. *Terribile!*

"Dante's *Inferno* captured the imagination of Auguste Rodin – whom many call the founder of modern sculpture – in much of his work. For example, *The Thinker* is Dante himself, contemplating. *The Gates of Hell* is an enormous work that took Rodin almost forty years to complete. *The Thinker* appears in *The Gates* as well; and *Ugolin et ses enfants* is a part of *The Gates*, as well as an independent piece. *Ugolin et ses enfants* is a plaster inside the Rodin Museum in Paris and one of the primary works, cast in bronze, in the middle of an ornamental pool in the Rodin Museum garden. I was fortunate to be able to contemplate all these works several times and for hours.

"As an amateur Dantista and a devotee of Rodin, this poem emerged."

[8] Thea Biesheuvel writes that her poem, 'Give It Time', "arose out of a news story that documented the wonderful advances that have been made in the treatment of *anorexia nervosa*, the mental state that propels people into a starvation diet, disliking food, even water at times and wasting away. This is very different to the involuntary starvation suffered by many across the globe, mainly in Africa and India, where people want to eat but can't access food and gradually lose the ability to digest food.

"In spite of the good intentions of the affluent nations to correct these conditions, neither of them seems to vanish. Our Western world seems at times to 'teach' us to become apathetic to all sorts of anguish and so to accept these as 'normal'. Even though the dignity and pride of the individuals and nations suffer as a result, it seems the rest of us can accept anything, given time."

[9] Thea Biesheuvel writes that her poem, 'Shades Of Hunger', "arose out of the poem she'd just constructed about our apathy and lack of sympathy with the suffering of others, and tackles this from a feeling that we are in a state of neglect.

"We have neglected those in need mostly, but we also neglect to care for our environment, our country. This leads us to neglect our loves as well. We grow ever more numb, our feelings seem to matter less and less. Eventually this will lead to a neglect of self. Our identity will lack a substance. A sense of self will empty out. We already have the 'skipping' of meals, the inability to cook. Nothing will colour our world. Soon we will be transparent ghosts, dimly remembering what great social events communal meals can provide. We can't recognise our neighbours, our social circle, and that will be the hunger that will ache the most."

[10] María Elena Blanco writes that her poem, 'Unusual Uses of the Time Zone', "was written in the early months of the COVID-19 pandemic, in May 2020, in Las Cruces, a small resort town facing the Pacific Ocean, the home, and now the burial place, of the long-lived (103)

Chilean creator of the so-called 'Anti-poetry' genre, Nicanor Parra (1914-2018).

"Las Cruces is situated on a coastal strip in central Chile between, a few miles to the north, the town of Isla Negra, home and burial place of Nobel Prize-winning poet Pablo Neruda (1904-1973) and, a bit further south, the town of Cartagena, home and last resting place of another important Chilean poet, Vicente Huidobro (1893-1948), the father of 'Creationism', a poetic movement of the Latin American avant-garde of the 1920s.

"No wonder this string of lazy, sandy beaches separated by stretches of capricious rock formations constantly swept by wind and sea foam is called the 'Poets' Coastline' ('Litoral de los Poetas')! And this is where I have been confined – to this day – during an unprecedented global crisis of a kind no one could imagine or was ready for on New Year's Day 2020.

"It turned out to be real confinement: months of not stepping out to the street other than to receive a food delivery left on the floor, by the outward fence, lifted with glove-clad hands and then disinfected thoroughly, with previous and subsequent self-sanitizing with alcohol gel or copious soap and water; constant attention to news of curves, casualties and further restrictions here and around the world, especially where there are relatives and friends, in other continents and time zones; sleepless nights and zombie-like days or, more likely, a combination of both.

"On one such night of sudden waking in the dark and being startled by peculiar shadows on the wall, murmurs and halos coming out of invisible objects, bright lights floating in the void, and haphazard thoughts of uncertainty and unease, futility and finitude rushing through my mind, I reached blindly for pen and paper from my night table and scribbled some words which became, late in the morning the next day, almost unchanged after some close-up deciphering, the poem 'Unusual Uses of the Time Zone'."

[11] Gavin Bourke explains that he wrote his poem, 'Unremarkable' earlier in the year. "It is, I suppose, without wishing to give too much away, a poem about ordinary, everyday life and about ordinary everyday human suffering. I tend to have a narrative thread, or core, to my longer work and I wrap sometimes other ideas, images etc. around that core or trunk, so that I can address a lot of things, in contemporary and historical life, and connect the two. The point, I suppose, is that life is unremarkable overall, we are all passing through to some extent, bound by those parameters, although within that, I believe we should strive for an existence, in so far as is possible, where we do not harm

others and wish each other well. Life in itself, I believe, is unremarkable, part of the long continuum of creation, though each human life, ironically, is remarkable. We are remarkable and we should look out for each other!"

[12] Lawrence Bridges writes that his poem, 'The Farmer That You Recommended', "is a meditation on the past, a recognition that there are two 'pasts', one behind us that recedes forever, and another past, that sliver of time in which we take action just milliseconds before the present becomes our history, where pleasure and joy reside."

[13] Paul Brooke writes, "'Gwsberys' is an overtly political poem and based on the rhyme scheme found in the Welsh form gwawdodyn, a four-line stanza with 9, 9, 10 and 9 syllables. I came up with the idea for the poem when I saw a Welsh saying, 'Chwynnwch eich gardd eich hun yn gyntaf,' which means, 'weed your own garden first.' Essentially, fix yourself first before becoming too radicalized and losing touch with reality. *Rhagfarn* is Welsh for 'prejudice.' I was critiquing the American political system as the right was becoming very violent toward the left – and now has stormed the Capitol – but this could apply to any political system in any region or country."

[14] Lina Buividavičiūtė writes, "Almost all my poetry, including, 'Apathy (The Heaviness of the Hand)', is close to the confessional genre. This particular poem is from the special cycle, 'Syndroms' (which I plan to publish in my second book). I write about different mental disorders, syndromes and difficult states of mind. I am faced with depression and anxiey, so I think I have the experience to talk about it. I wanted to show what is under this mental disorder, to go deep in it. I know and experience apathy as a symptom of depression. Another thing I want to emphasize is that depression impacts the whole life of the sufferer, his relationships with others and the world. The mood of this poem is full of desperation, resignation and a bit of hope. I wanted to use symbols and images to emphasize the difficulty and darkness of apathy."

[15] Lina Buividavičiūtė writes, "Almost all my poetry, including, 'Not Getting The Nobel', is close to the genre of confessional poetry. It is based on personal experience but I always want to fill the poem not only with personal meanings, but with universal symbols, images, meanings as well. To talk about this specific poem – it is based on a true story. Once I was sitting next to my psychotherapist and crying because I will never get the Nobel prize... I wanted to emphasize the

importance and pain of desperate seeking for glory, attention and victories. I really believe this moment – sitting and crying in the psychotherapist's office – is only an outcome, a consequence which has a reason. By means of this poem I wanted to ask a question – what happened in the poem subject's life, in his childhood, that he so desperately wants to win, to get all prizes... And the value of his life is based only on prizes, victories... I wanted to put strong emotions in this poem – anger, desperation and a lot of irony."

[16] Paola Caronni tells us that her poem, 'Out in the World' responds to the theme of Hunger (in this case 'Hunger for Knowledge'). "After nearly nineteen years of living together as a family of four, in late August 2019 my children left Hong Kong for University, one to Los Angeles and one to Vancouver. To have them both leave at the same time was for me heart-breaking, even if I fully supported their decision to be 'out in the world' alone, in order to experience it fully, to satisfy their hunger for knowledge and their desire for new experiences.

"My poem 'Out in the World' talks to them, wishing them to find nurturing in their new places, to get to know other realities, get acquainted with different cultures, tasting the ups and downs of the human experience. All this, while I struggle with the sixteen-hour time difference and the constant thought that, here in Asia, I am always almost one day ahead of them, as if I lived in the future and they, in the past. This leaves me suspended in a surreal dimension, with 'an hour that I keep on chasing so that it ticks with mine'.

"Ultimately, the cycle of Nature and of the Earth still marks our day. The sun remains our guide, and my wish is for my children to cherish its presence so that, despite life's challenges, it could brighten their paths each and every day, wherever they will decide to be."

[17] Anne Casey elaborates on her poem, 'Night Traps'. "As a former environment journalist, an author and a mother, I worry greatly about the state of our precious planet and what we will leave behind for our children. Ecopolitics features large in my poetry and other writing.

"This narrative poem tells the story of my struggle as a mother to grapple with my children's anxieties around climate change and the human activities that are wreaking havoc on Earth.

"I and my family are blessed to live on the edge of a natural reserve, teeming with native Australian wildlife, where we go bushwalking. This is sadly under threat due to State government development plans; our community protests have fallen on deaf ears.

"As a family, we also love snorkelling and observing the abundant and extraordinary indigenous marine life, particularly around the Great

Barrier Reef. Again, this is in imminent danger due to the impacts of human activities. My younger son, in particular, shares my passion for the bountiful gifts of nature and he has had many sleepless nights worrying about his beloved animal friends."

[18] Ian Chambers gives the background to his poem, 'At Yeats' Grave'. "Whilst on a trip to Sligo I visited the grave of famous Irish poet W.B. Yeats. He is buried in a small church in the shadow of Benbulben, an iconic local mountain. By the time I reached the church it was getting dark and when I found his grave it was illuminated by the faint glow of the church lights. The surrounding darkness and a star-studded night sky reinforced a feeling of human insignificance in the universal scheme of things. Yeats was interested in spiritualism and I wondered whether his creative 'essence' – whatever it was that made him special whilst alive – could indeed survive death, and if not, then sadly his earthly contributions would, in the end, be of no more consequence than my own."

[19] Ian Chambers writes as follows about, 'Grandma's Dilemma'. "If you are lucky enough to have photographs and/or documents from your ancestors it can help you to put yourself in their shoes and try to gain some understanding of what their life was like and the impact it may have had on your own life. Growing up in Australia, I had little contact with my father's mother in the north of England and after she and my father had both passed away, I came into possession of information that showed that she had placed him in an orphanage, something I was driven to try to understand. In a strange way, the constraints of the poem's pantoum structure seemed to complement the stark imagery and eliminate any familial romanticism."

[20] Of the poem, 'Hunger', Josie Chambers writes, "I'm trying to compress all those times when we feel empathy for other people – recognising their hunger – for food perhaps, for comfort, for security, warmth, love – but we find ways of telling ourselves that there's nothing we can do to help. After all, we are told not to give to those who beg on the street, because it will not help them – they will just spend the money on drugs or alcohol. Of course, that may be true – but when we 'pass by' that is, I think we know, not just a rational decision – it's a way of pushing other people's needs to the back of our minds – and it may be a way of saying to ourselves, 'I'm hungry too'."

[21] Writing of, 'Of, by and for the People', Josie Chambers writes, "In Abraham Lincoln's 1863 Gettysburg Address, he identified a 'great

task remaining before us,' calling on people to dedicate themselves to working for 'a new birth of freedom' to ensure 'that government of the people, by the people, for the people, shall not perish from the earth'. This poem was prompted by an increasing feeling that – all over our world – this task still remains before us. Wherever we live, It seems that we need to search urgently for ways of living together that enable us to share responsibility, hear each other, acknowledge our debts to each other and find ways of caring for those of us who are in need."

[22] Jessica Chan explains references in her poem, 'Withdrawing Us'. "June 2019 saw the escalation of protests asking for the withdrawal of an anti-extradition bill in Hong Kong. Sogo is a shopping mall at the heart of the Causeway Bay district on Hong Kong Island."

[23] Commenting on his poem, 'Pickled Chicken's Feet', Kwan Ee Chan writes, "While there are the more common (and popular) types of food in Hong Kong like *dim sum* and *siu mai*, there are also strange ones, and they are equally representational of the food culture of Hong Kong: to eat everything from chicken's feet to snake stew, an extreme search for exotic foods. But then there are the ordinary foods (or poor-people food), which we grew up with and hold dear. We always look forward to that piece of salted egg served with rice. Whether it's strange or bland or perhaps it just simply tastes/looks awful to others, it is the sentiment that gives it taste."

[24] Carol Flake Chapman writes as follows about her poem, 'Sequestered Sunday'. "When I learned that the theme for the next Proverse contest would be hunger, I began thinking about different kinds of hunger, and in particular, about the ceremony that my native American ancestors practiced, and which I have practiced myself: the vision quest. During the vision quest, the individual goes out alone in a spot in nature and fasts for a period of time, which is also a time of soul-searching. In a sense, for many of us, the sequestering that we observe during the corona virus pandemic has been a kind of vision quest, as we seclude ourselves and think about what we truly value. The solitude, in that sense, can bring us to a new awareness of how we want to live our lives. I thought also of the monarch butterflies, which undergo a period of sequestering in their chrysalis and emerge with a new life."

[25] Cheng Tim Tim writes that the poem, 'Gnaw', "is a response to Hong Kong's urban, linguistic and political environments. Born and raised in Hong Kong, I always find it an overgrown and worn-out place

with missing details. Since my teenage years, I developed an escapism
from its density and tension – writing in my second language, English,
at the expense of my written Chinese. The unrest in 2020, locally and
globally, created an urge in me to devour every piece of news on my
feed. I was particularly fascinated by Hong Kongers' increasing
attention to the Sandy Ridge cemetery for unidentified bodies. I
wondered if new discoveries always entail the death of something."

[26] Annie Christain, 'Now That You're Well Fed In Love'.
<u>Note from Annie Christain</u>
"The mountains melt beneath him and the valleys split apart, like wax
before the fire, like water rushing down a slope." (Micah 1:4)

[27] William Leo Coakley explains that the title of his poem, 'An
Immovable Feast', " is a play on the term 'Moveable Feast' used in the
Christian religion for holy days like Easter, celebrated on a different
day each year, and also used by Ernest Hemingway for a book about
Paris. Paris after World War Two took a very long time to recover and
it was not till the 1960s that some of the beautiful ancient building like
the royal palace of the Louvre or the French Academy which face the
Seine were cleaned of their accumulated grime and restored to the
original almost golden limestone. For years many vagrants
called *clochard*s often slept along the Seine, sometimes a man and a
woman together."

[28] William Leo Coakley writes about his poem, 'Ashes'. "There are
many Chinese art collections in New York where I live. I love seeing
the water-colours, prints, sculpture, and ceramics, especially the floral
vases of the Song Dynasty. Since my youth, I have been greatly
influenced by the great T'ang poets. "Recently, several friends have
died, some of them cremated. One of them, a lovely woman, had had
famous lovers when she was young. I was thinking of what would have
been an appropriate receptacle for her ashes and a Song vase seemed
one that would be right. Then I thought about the possibility that it had
been originally presented to a courtesan at the court of a Song
emperor."

[29]   Suzanne Cottrell explains that she chose the title, 'Cast Iron
Mothers,' "because a cast iron skillet is a mainstay of a farm kitchen
and is known for its durability." She continues, "In the mid-1930s, the
U. S. Farm Security Administration commissioned Dorothea Lange, an
American photographer, to document the impact of federal programs
on farming communities during the Great Depression. In March 1936,

she photographed migrant workers near Nipomo, California, after severe weather had damaged the pea crop. One of Lange's most iconic photographs was of an unidentified migrant mother sheltering her children. The mother became a symbol of poverty and hunger, as well as of courage, strength, and maternal sacrifice. It wasn't until 1978 that readers learned the identity of the migrant mother, Florence Owens Thompson. I wanted to write a poem comparing the hardships and resiliency of 'The Migrant Mother' with those of contemporary single mothers.

"The Jackson Street Bridge in Atlanta, Georgia, is also iconic. From the top of the bridge is the picturesque skyline view of the city; whereas, beneath the bridge, many of the city's homeless seek shelter."

[30] Neil Douglas tells us that his poem, 'Breakfast Buffet', was composed during a stay at Discovery Bay on Lantau Island, Hong Kong and explains that it is, "written as a pair of haikus and can be taken as a commentary on choice in modern relationships".

[31] As for his poem, 'Chalybeate Spring', Neil Douglas explains that this a freshwater spring in Kent, England. "The water has high iron content and is famed for its therapeutic properties for a range of maladies. The poem is written in sonnet form and addresses the expectation of 'cure' from medicinal treatments."
<u>Editor's note</u>
Selene: goddess of the Moon

[32] Neil Douglas explains that his poem, 'Man-made Shirt', was written for a friend and is, "about genetics and the characteristics we inherit from both parents to make ourselves a composite person".

[33] Neil Douglas explains that his poem, 'Suburban Crescent', "has the Moon as a voyeuristic participant in domestic shenanigans in an urban English suburb and is shaped to suggest both the appearance of the moon and adjacent houses in a cul-de-sac."

[34] Neil Douglas writes that his poem, 'The Bus', is, "about the unpredictability of Life (and death) and reflects my work as a GP [General Practitioner, i.e. a medical doctor] and the dilemma of juggling patient beliefs and expectations with science and the management of uncertainty."
<u>Editor's note</u>
"pop your clogs" (informal): to die

³⁵ Neil Douglas wrote, 'the doctor is a ship's pilot', "for a GP colleague, Dr Jo Richardson, to mark her retirement. The free form without punctuation reflects the doctor's navigation of a working life which has multiple, seemingly random demands and dimensions which are connected by underlying compassion."

³⁶ Gayathri Durairaj writes, "The poem 'Water and Power' was written at the height of the Hong Kong protests. As an expat in Hong Kong, all I could do was just helplessly look on. Just be an observer of an ongoing political cause.

"I live on the south side of Hong Kong island just opposite the beach, so the sea and water have given me a lot of inspiration to write. In this case they provided an analogy: the protesters were water and the brute force showed on them was fire. In the poem, I've broached the feeling of people's unity and identity and also hinted at the silent forces at play and the shock waves it sent through the international community.

"Struggle in every political situation anywhere always leaves remnants of the strife and chaos and it takes a while to pick up the broken pieces. Sometimes, the thoughts and ideas of a long cause fade into wishful illusions."

³⁷ Ahmed Elbeshlawy, wrote 'Carcass on a Bed' in April 2020. He writes, "I believe the writing was affected by two events happening separately in the same week; discussing necrophilia with two of my HKU SPACE students and seeing an old love (unrequited love), after thirty years of separation, on a social media platform. The poem came out of mixed images of the young woman from memory, the present virtual middle-aged one, the imagined future elderly one and the imagined corpse. The enjoyment of poetic creativity, which matches the enjoyment of making love, is mixed with the enjoyment of the memory or the imagined sizes, shapes and colours of all the objects that provided – or would have provided – the context for making love, which never took place in reality, and thus, resembles making love to ghosts, or alternative women, or the imagined corpse of the beloved, who – typically – wouldn't give herself while still alive."

³⁸ Ahmed Elbeshlawy writes that his poem, 'Grief', "is inspired by a recurring idea which is represented in numerous cinematic scenes – that of making love as if it is a matter of life or death, or indulging in an act of desperately passionate sexual intercourse, while in a fresh state of mourning, right after the loss of a dear person, in particular, a mother or a father. In real life, I have personally experienced this twice. It was

guilt-ridden, terrific, and traumatizing. It establishes a connection between sexuality and death, and proves that human beings do not want to be simply alive, but to enjoy life to excess, beyond the ordinary run of things – and excess always leads to death."

[39] Fetūolemoana Elisara tell us that her poem, 'Wishing I Could YeLL for my Mother', "is a tribute to my nine-year-old self. Sad statistics reveal that one in four girls, and one in six boys will be sexually abused before they turn eighteen and that the majority of abusers will be a family member."

[40] D. W. Evans writes that, although his poem, 'Goodbye Stranger', "is not a linear account of a hit and run, elements of my experience of finding an injured dog in roadside undergrowth are true. As is the moribund fact that the dog died. We tried to calm her – myself and some other boys –whether we were successful or not is lost to time, I'd like to hope we were. This was many years ago, and the poem hints that the scene is not a contemporary one. For example, the reference to Bess, her puppies and the awful drowning of these whelps places us firmly in the last century. Sterilisation of dogs and cats in the 1960s and 1970s was unusual, the procedure was costly and few could afford a veterinarian's fee for this operation.

"Responsible owners would, therefore, apply preventive measures, such as keeping their pets indoors if they were in *heat*; a sensible precaution, but hardly a fool-proof one.

"The reader shouldn't run away with the notion that the River Tyne (a major river in the north east of England) was clogged and turbulent with small mammals struggling for life in weighted sacks. Disposing of small animals in this way was bad business back then, but it did happen, much to the distress of children and of course the animals themselves."

Notes from D. W. Evans

"pitman": The reference to pitman also places the narrative in the previous century. "Pitman" in this context refers to a coalminer, and "the pitman's side" to a portion of village housing originally provided by the National Coal Board which, post industrialisation, reverted to local authority housing stock.

"The Green": a village green, originally common grazing land and latterly a recreation ground, sometimes given over to intra-village sports competitions, fetes and fairs.

"Bairn": an interchangeable noun between Scotland and the North East of England, meaning a young child or children.

[41] Adele Evershed writes that her poem, 'A Crown for All the "Gone to China" Girls', "was inspired by my time living in Singapore. I had taken a tour of the Japanese Cemetery Park during which I learnt about the 'Karayuki-san', buried there. They were Japanese women sold into prostitution and sent to Singapore from about 1880 to 1940. The women were from mainly poor rural backgrounds, some were unwanted daughters, some were tricked by the promise of work in rubber plantations and some were kidnapped. What I found of particular interest was that they were buried in a cemetery on land donated by three Japanese brothel keepers and many of their tombstones had no name and were turned away from Japan. I read that it was so the families back in Japan would not suffer embarrassment if their daughters' fate were known. Many of the images in the poem are drawn from my time in Singapore. The bamboo poles hanging from windows to dry washing are a common sight. Likewise for anyone who has lived in Singapore or Hong Kong the unique smell of the durian fruit that fills streets during 'durian season' is very familiar. A 'paper bark tree' is also known as 'Gelam' and is found in various countries in Asia. It has whitish bark that, according to *Wild Singapore*, 'may peel off in large flakes like sheets of paper'. The phrase, 'sheeted in snow,' refers to the white kimono that would be the traditional Japanese burial garment."

[42] <u>Notes from Ryan Fenton</u>
Ye Si: pen name of Leung Ping-kwan (1949-2013), Hong Kong poet, scholar, and cultural figure.
North Point: an area of Hong Kong Island.

[43] Daniela Fischerová writes that her poem 'Self-Portrait with the Mirror and the Moth' ('Autoportrét se zrcadlem a molem'), "is from the collection entitled *Potvora mlsná* ('Greedy Beast', 2020). An old woman is standing in the empty house of her mind, where barely anything is left. The image in the mirror frightens her, because she no longer recognises herself. The text is as bare and errant as the situation itself. Alzheimer is one of my most profound fears. I'm not afraid of covid or of cancer, but of losing personality and memory."

[44] Lincoln Greenhaw writes this about his poem 'Preservation at Byblos'. "Forty kilometers north of Beirut, Lebanon, among new beach clubs playing loud house music, the Byblos Port is still open. This is the place from which the Greeks received papyrus for writing. There is a stone restaurant and fishing club where Brigitte Bardot often stayed, and not far away the ruins of a castle from the time of the crusades

stand out above collapsed temples and the disparate versions of a town that has been rebuilt on the edges of the windy beach for the last nine thousand years. During our two years teaching in Lebanon, I often watched my girlfriend, Anamika, take sea pictures on cliffs there, near the ruins. The town had a civic character that seemed to become almost supernatural as daily business connected historical sites that people were trying to maintain. This poem was written in humility at seeing an underground tomb preserved near the market and at seeing what so many years of feet have done to stairs there."

[45] Casey Hampton writes that the poem, 'A Taste of Loneliness', "speaks to the paradox of reaching for what we cannot reach, and having that define one's existence. When I wrote this poem, I was attempting to reconcile feelings of grief and desire with the past and with the present. All this is to say, I was trying to find my way."

[46] Kate Hawkins explains that her poem, '4 Knocks', "is about choosing another path, not opening a door both literally and figuratively, and trusting ones instinct in an uncomfortable situation."

[47] Kate Hawkins tells us that her poem, 'I Do, Hunger For You', was, "written in the aftermath of the ending of a long-term relationship, and the coming to terms of what will never be. Written in the form of a poetic interpretation of wedding vows for a couple whose paths have gone separate ways, into separate futures. It is a poem of lost love."

[48] Ching Yee Ho writes, "For 'Artist Abstract', I was largely inspired by my own experiences with writing. I wanted to highlight the process of creating and looking at art, and of having constantly to negotiate with different layers of authenticity while doing so. There will be instances where I can only replicate an emotion or experience that I have never lived through. In this case, I may not have suffered so much from hunger that I never knew when my next meal would come. I wondered if this was problematic.

"I wanted then to portray honestly the process of creating art and to provide multiple perspectives in my poem, perspectives of both the artist and his subject. I intended to emphasise how creating any piece of art requires a sort of skewed vision. Yet even if the artist may have this skewed vision, this in itself offers additional perspectives for the audience, as we draw multiple interpretations from not only the artwork but how it is portrayed.

"By portraying the sometimes problematic process of art-making, I hoped to challenge myself and to suggest how art never exists as an isolated subject. I try to bring to light these thoughts, and hopefully by revealing my own experiences I can be one step closer to understanding the world around me."

[49] Kathy Hoa writes this about her poem, 'My Mind Is Hungry'. "What I really wanted to express in this poem is how severe depression manifests in my life. I wanted to use the analogy of a hungry spirit akin to a demon or monster and how it feeds on the things that I want to achieve. I think in that way my poem is very relatable because when you are in such a negative place it's hard to have hope and see positivity in life. Another thing I wanted to comment on, is what I say in stanza 4 about it being worse at night. For me, nights are terrifying because I'm left alone with my thoughts and it takes a toll on my sleep. That's why this poem ends on such a dark note because not only is this hungry spirit taking away my ambition but it is affecting my overall health. There's nothing glamorous about depression and I wanted to express that in this poem."

[50] Joshua Ip writes, "The poem, 'the accusation of the banana bread', was written during the circuit-breaker partial lockdown/quarantine of Singapore in the middle of 2020 and the outbreak of the COVID-19 pandemic. During this period, many Singaporeans began to engage in baking as a way to avert boredom during quarantine, and provide themselves homemade calorie-rich sustenance. This effort was aggravated by social media envy of lovingly-photographed crust and texture, and retarded by an island-wide shortage of baking supplies. The poem reflects on these phenomena, and the almost-religious, hopeful aspects of the oven ritual and its transformative, redemptive potential during these dark times."

[51] Joshua Ip writes that his poem, 'the master never reveals the 18th stroke', "is an extended reflection that grew out of a discussion with Chng Kai Fong on GPT-3 and the ability of AI to copy and imitate, set against the still-unmapped ability of the human mind for abstract inspiration – how the ink paintings of Chua Ek Kay evoke the concept of fractals, and how the concepts of mushin no shin, unconscious competence etc. still provide some faint hope for human mastery, the legendary 18th stroke that may one day be passed on to our AI trainees, or not…"

Notes from Joshua Ip
"the master never reveals the 18th stroke": a longstanding trope in martial arts novels / dramas / films, where a wary kungfu master passes

on only a percentage of his skills to his disciples, often keeping one or two ultimate moves for himself to safeguard his masterhood. This usually foments distrust among his disciples and the eventual decline of the martial arts sect in question as their repertoire of skills diminishes over time.

mushin no shin (無心の心): "mind of no-mind", or a mental state of "no-mindness" that martial artists and Zen meditators endeavor to reach – comparable to the contemporary, "flow".

"they know not what they do": a reference to Luke 23:34 of the Christian bible, where Jesus asks for forgiveness for those who crucified him. The ensuing section is also an extended riff / response to W. H. Auden's "Musée des Beaux Arts": "About suffering they were never wrong, / The old Masters…"

"beyond the point of unconscious competence… petered unprincipled": the peter principle is the idea that every employee rises through the hierarchy of an organisation until reaching their level of incompetence. Unconscious competence is also probably the organisational literature equivalent of mushin no shin.

"kata": (型) or "form", a set of martial arts movements for practice and internalization.

[52] 'Ties'
Note
"de clieu": a coffee shop chain

[53] Sadie Kaye writes, "'War of Voices' is my first poem and my first attempt at not using humor as armour (or a weapon). It muses on issues related to mental health, social media (tribalism versus marginalization), populism and propaganda. It is inspired by our rapacious hunger to be heard and validated, and by the idea that, by refusing to acknowledge any self-awareness, we are merely throwing up half-digested information or obvious propaganda, thus doing inevitable damage to our mental health and core identity.

"Although I wrote the poem during the early part of the Hong Kong Protests, before they turned violent and well before the introduction of the National Security Law, nobody knew then where they were going to lead. So although some of the themes that 'War of Voices' explores may seem particularly pertinent in the current political maelstrom, the poem is actually a philosophical comment on the wider issues of the Age of Intolerance and Information Overload. In particular, it's about the division of communities in the West over political lines and how rational and empathetic debate has been stifled by the growth of social media and the willful spread of misinformation online. It reflects on the irony that something that was created to help the spread of human connection has resulted in more division, not less. Our need to seek validation from strangers online contradicts the much-vaunted growth of 'individualism', suggesting it is perhaps just another empty and narcissistic label we use to define ourselves – something that I often find myself pondering in the wee hours. The ending highlights the importance of tuning out the white noise of warring voices whenever they threaten to consume our core being, by disconnecting from our digital devices in order to reconnect with ourselves (and each other) in real time.

"Mental health is a cause very close to my heart and the subject of two documentaries I have produced & presented for RTHK Radio 3, 'Bipolar Express' and 'As Bad As It Gets'. In 2020 I produced & presented a series of 12 podcasts, which have aired on RTHK Radio 3's '123 Show', exploring innovative approaches to tackling mental health in an entertaining, provocative and accessible way. I also co-produced my first narrative feature film, 'Transference: A Bipolar Love Story', which was shortlisted for and won several international film festivals. I was diagnosed with bipolar disorder in 2011, but don't view my condition as a disability. I use it as a tool to fuel my creativity, spark lively debate, help spread mental health awareness, and provide support and opportunities for others. I have set up and run two local nonprofit groups, Bipolar Hong Kong and Mental Ideas, to help Hongkongers with mental illness channel emotions that are hard to voice creatively and share stories and artwork in an empowering and inclusive environment."

[54] R. J. Keeler writes, "The first draft of my poem 'My Mind Is Out To Kill Me' was written on 5/11/2018. I wrote twenty more revisions until the last one, written on 5/4/2020.

"A part of the back story, but perhaps not the entire one, is that in April 2018, just one month before the first draft, my beloved dog Izzy died of complications from diabetes. I was somewhat culpable in her death because I did not take all possible measures in her last days to keep her alive. When I look back on that time, I was both peculiarly fuzzy in my thinking and lacking in good decision-making capability. I don't really know why I was so affected.

"But, out of this strange lapse in mental capability, over the coming months, I began to write the poem around the theme of the strangeness of the human brain, somewhat as I had experienced it just a month beforehand. I was also a bit angry at myself for my stupid participation in Izzy's death.

"I guess at the end the two themes came together: anger at my mental failures and curiosity at how strange the functioning of the human brain can be. So out of this mix came a poem that incorporated both the strangeness and wonder of the brain, and the anger at myself."

[55] Lynda McKinney Lambert submits the following mission statement: "1) Seeking Euphoria, through my art and writing; 2) I reveal what is forgotten, lost or invisible".

She writes this about, 'A Spring-Cleaned Poem'. "From my earliest memories, spring-cleaning is a tradition that begins every year in March.

"In our Germanic tradition, I learned at an early age that spring is for cleaning the house from top to bottom, every nook and cranny, drawer, and closet.

"This tradition inspired me to write my poem this year. It was my second poem created on the second day of National Poetry Month. Each year I try to write poems as a way of celebrating this month-long poetry event. I chose the Tritina form to provide the structure to begin my poetic Spring Cleaning. Tritina – a 20th-century poem form – provided me with the space I needed to compose my story through poetry."

[56] Lynda McKinney Lambert writes of her poem, 'Boxing Day'. "First, this is a holiday that is not observed in the USA, so I was thinking about it and did some research into the holiday. It really is not anything I've ever heard anyone here in the USA mentioning, so I was curious to learn more.

"For the past six years I selected one word that I would focus on for an entire year. The word for 2020 is 'Gifts.'

"After I selected this word, I read an end-of-the-year challenge given by Indian-American visual artist, Sara Joseph. In her Christmas Newsletter she asks her readers to think of everything we do this year as a special gift for God, the King. I thought about how I would approach my art works and my writings this year, with that in mind. How would I choose to do everything if I was making it for the King? How would it make a difference in everything I create? This poem is an exploration of those thoughts."

[57] Lynda McKinney Lambert writes this about her poem, 'Portrait of a Virgo Girl'. "Because I am a visual artist, I am accustomed to seeing my art works on the walls of a gallery or museum. I've exhibited my work extensively since the late 1970s, and I am a retired Professor of Fine Art and Humanities. "It was just natural for me to think of telling my personal history as if I was standing in a gallery looking at a picture on the wall. This is where I begin.

"For National Poetry Month, I was asked to partner with the poet, Carrie Hooper, and do a presentation of our poetry and our lives as poets. We decided that each of us would write a story-poem that would share our ancestry as an introduction. This is the poem I created for that purpose. We called these our personal history poems.

"This poem is a self-portrait that shares aspects of my heritage and my ancestry. I appear in the poem as the poet, the artist, and the viewer."

[58] Lynda McKinney Lambert explains as follows about her poem, 'Preparations for a Virtual Spring Salad'. "In celebration of National Poetry Month, I was invited to participate in a virtual celebration that would be in the format of a luncheon. I loved the idea of celebrating together in this way.

"Each poet would bring a poem that would be one of the delightful food options for our virtual luncheon together. I chose to bring a salad because I am a vegetarian. I wanted to write about the variety of vegetables as a metaphor for the variety of parts of speech in a poem. I wanted it to be a large and expansive poem – because it is important to me to share my love of poetry, language, and friendship with other poets in our virtual gathering.

"I wrote this poem to tell a story of planting, gathering, harvesting, preserving , and dining on the food as a GIFT from the earth."

[59] Lynda McKinney Lambert wrote her acrostic poem, 'Scatterings', on May 26, 2020. "It is an exploration of my feelings and a response to the world-wide Covid-19 virus that has affected everyone.

"Unless we have a medical background, we are now speaking words that we never spoke or thought about before this year. Who ever thought of having a conversation with a friend which would produce toxic 'droplets'? We talk about being 'shut-down' and such ideas as 'toxic environmental productions.'

"People are expressing feelings of fear and despair caused by this sickness that is invisible. It is a kind of 'scattering' experienced all around the world in 2020.

"We feel disconnected from others because of social distancing and fear of getting sick.

"Writing this poem helped me focus on my own thoughts about what is happening in my own little spot on the planet."

[60] <u>Note from Lynda McKinney Lambert</u> on her poem, 'The Dry Landscape Garden (*karesansui*)':
"hojo": a reference to the Hojo gardens – and porch – at a temple in Japan. A place where we sit and look over our garden day and night – we are watchers of this place, like the red-tailed hawks which appear in the beginning of the poem.

[61] Lee Ho Cheung writes that he does not want to reveal too much about his poem, 'Before I Noticed It', "as the verse has taken a more implicit style to recount a simple household matter. But what triggered me to write this verse was the day when I returned home and found that some 'hardware' installed somewhere in the apartment had been changed. I thought it must have gone through a complicated process. It is funny to notice that there are so many things in our lives that are changing every day without our knowing, let alone all the hard work behind those changes."

[62] Lee Ho Cheung explains that his poem, 'To The Boy Who Smashed My Windscreen', is "An exploration of love and hatred. I asked myself the following question before I composed this verse: 'What if my best friend, whom I trusted with my life, betrayed me?' The narrator in this verse seems to have had such an experience of a heartbreaking broken relationship, so hurtful that the love immediately becomes a curse. I think this malicious revengeful feeling does not only occur between lovers, but very close friends as well."

[63] J.P. Linstroth explains that his poem, 'Boarding Up My Heart', "Is loosely based upon the Native American boarding school experiences of Dennis Banks (1937-2017), Ojibwe (*Nowa Cumig*), co-founder of the American Indian Movement (AIM) and Native American activist. See Interview for Documentary, 'What They Took Away: Reflections on Native Boarding Schools' (2015):
https://www.youtube.com/watch?v=ZO38EUu-1uA
See also the documentary, 'Unspoken: America's Native American Boarding Schools', PBS (2016):
https://www.youtube.com/watch?v=Yo1bYj-R7F0 And also the following documentary:
https://www.youtube.com/watch?v=ioAzggmes8c

There are also many books on this subject.

"The Native American boarding schools lasted from the 19th century until at least the 1970s and were responsible for generations of Native peoples being traumatized in the United States and Canada. Native children were forcibly removed from their Native homes and placed in boarding schools, separating Native children from their families. It was a history of 'forced assimilation'. In many cases, Natives were ridiculed for being Indian and were taught 'not' to speak their Native tongues and that their Native cultures were inferior to white culture. A common refrain was: 'Kill the Indian, Save the Man' from Captain Richard H. Pratt in 1892. Their Native beliefs and traditions were replaced with Christian values. In many Native boarding schools, Native children were sexually abused and in some cases by nuns and priests. Such institutions continued the 'genocidal policies' against Native peoples of Canada and the United States. See information from the National Museum of the American Indian: https://americanindian.si.edu/education/codetalkers/html/chapter3.html Also, see: https://www.history.com/news/how-boarding-schools-tried-to-kill-the-indian-through-assimilation"

[64] Iris Litt writes, "I once had an urge to tell the story of my life very briefly, with just symbols, of very important events. Here it is, in 'Taking Stock'. But the last line brings us beyond to absolute reality: 'On the other hand, the children and the trees grew, and they all used to ask me if I'd lost my tongue and that's still wagging.' What is more real than children and trees and one's desire to communicate through human speech?"

[65] Sharon E. Ludan writes, "My back story for 'To the Universe' is fairly straightforward. In fact I thought of including a sub-title, 'Upon Reaching a Certain Age, the Poet Addresses a Letter to the Universe'. It's about reaching a certain stage in life, a crossroads, the end of one chapter and beginning of the next...although one doesn't quite know what the next episode will be, so one must just step to the edge of the known and leap into the unknown."

[66] K B Ryan Joshua Mahindapala writes this about his poem, 'The Computer Has Decided! The Computer Has Decided!'. "I was inspired to write this poem during the period of lockdown in Singapore caused by the deeply unfortunate circumstances brought about by the rapid spread of COVID-19 around the world. During that time, my MBA course with the University of Strathclyde went fully online. I was taking the "Information Technology Management" module which I

really enjoyed because it opened my mind to the possibilities of the many uses of technology, its application into different contexts and how it is changing the world. The marvellous thing was that I was learning about technology from books and articles, but I was also witnessing and experiencing first-hand its drastic impact. This was because COVID-19 caused a major surge in the use of technology and people have become more reliant on it to function on a daily basis. This got me thinking.

"When reading out the title, we fall into the trap of adopting a robotic tone due to the repetition of the same phrase, twice. It almost sounds like an automatic voice message that you hear when you make a phone call and there is no answer. This, really, is the essence of the poem. The poem is about computers taking over the world and overpowering humans. The fact that our natural inclination to read out the title in a robotic tone just shows how much computers have already taken a grip over our lives. It has affected our very thoughts, the way we speak and how we communicate with one another. No doubt, digitization will consume us completely in the future, and it will sap our free will. We are unable to fully comprehend this concept except to accept that it is inevitable.

"With the rampant spread of COVID-19, our reliance on technology has become even greater. Like a drug addict that cannot sustain without a hit, humans will soon find that not a minute can go by without them using some form of technology. It is sustenance, humans can't function without it. We are subservient to technology. The computer will be just as important as the air that we breathe. In fact, it already might be. We just have not realised it yet. Without it, there is no hope for the future although the irony is that technology is what got us into this mess in the first place and we, humans, were the ones that created it using our own supposedly superior ingenuity and intellect. We have put ourselves in this position. The future is uncertain, but one thing is for sure, humans will no longer be decision-makers. We will become prey. At the mercy of some artificially created being. What then is the justification for our existence if we are no longer in control?

"I think that no one will be spared. There are no innocent by-standers in this situation even if some of us may think that we are. The reality is that we share the burden of our existence equally, universally and we bear the consequences of our actions together, as a human race."

[67] During the lockdown in London, Carmina Masoliver joined a Facebook group, named 'Poetry London's in the time of being alone'. Her poem, 'A Portrait of The Hungry Caterpillar as a Body Positivity

Icon', she tells us, "Was inspired by a prompt to write a poem inspired by the children's book *The Hungry Caterpillar*. It was a book I grew up with and had fond memories of, and I had also studied it during my Children's Literature module at the University of East Anglia (UEA). At the time, I wrote another poem inspired by the book. This time, I put a positive spin on the book. Although the book was intended as having a message about healthy eating, I reinterpreted the story to be one about body positivity, aiming to take away any shame attached to the food eaten in the book and celebrating taking up space in a world that still tells women we should be small to be seen as beautiful."

[68] Wayne Paul Mattingly writes that his poem, 'Oedipus At The Acropolis', was, "inspired by a performance at The Acropolis I attended as a Theatre student with my college professor while on a three month tour of Europe. We sat a dozen or so rows back, and directly in front of us a Greek family of three were seated, left to right: Mother, Father and Daughter of about seventeen, with the latter directly in front of me. During the course of the performance, the young girl first merely leaned back against my knees for support, and as the drama unfolded, became more and more comfortable, leaning in, between, and eventually draping her arms over my legs as if armrests. I was both titillated and frightened – her father might at any moment take notice. He didn't. The music of the applause swept over us like rain falling on a lake, both she and I risen, then speaking our separate languages while the soft sounds of hands coming together fell silent all around us. I never saw her face nor she mine. When I wrote about this years later I switched the play to Oedipus, which I'd been studying and performing and so knew much better at the time of writing. In reality, we'd seen *The Bacchae*."

Notes from Wayne Paul Mattingly

Both the spacing and capitalization are as intended. Because this is a dramatic poem, or poem about a drama, I exercised a lot of control if you were to read it aloud.

The penultimate line in the first stanza also is as intended. As a dramatic moment every Greek and tourist was anticipating, I slurred that expectation into Oedipus' name and hopefully brought it to somewhat of a dramatic pause (break, halt) by placing it at the end of the line, enhanced by the plosive syllabic rhyme (pus/Puts).

[69] Wayne Paul Mattingly writes that his poem, 'Whistling Zombie', was, "Inspired by a true event that took place on one of my middle-age birthdays. I had taken a day off to bicycle in rural Connecticut and passed a field of grazing Herefords. Since I first learned when I was six

that St Francis of Assisi talked with the birds, I've been engaging them. However, having given up on spoken word to birds long ago, I shifted into whistling and mimicry, with fair resulting response. So, when I set my bicycle against the fence and approached the cows, I had no idea the attentive response I'd receive to my whistling. And who knew 'Zombie' would be such an attractive tune?"

[70] Jack Mayer writes that he, "composed 'False Labour' while hiking alone on Vermont's Long Trail, a wilderness trail that winds 273 miles down the spine of the Green Mountains. I have walked these mountains for more than 50 years. This poem reflects my thoughts about mortality and the provocative connection between birth and death. Physics teaches us that energy and matter are never destroyed, only change form. We are all resurrected in the reshuffling of our atoms after death – a rebirth. This poem suggests similarities between birth and death and the inevitability of both. 'False labour' – so-called Braxton-Hicks contractions – is an early sign of the birth process. I, too, feel the inevitable contractions of my demise, another kind of labour. (As a pediatrician, I have witnessed thousands of women in labour. I wonder if the fetus, in its birth struggles, does not feel that it, too is dying.)"

[71] The idea behind Maya Mitova's poem, 'Notesheet From The Dawn Of The Light', cane, as she explains, "on New Year's Eve – December 31. I was in Thessaloniki, Greece in front of the fortress in the old town, Ano Poli. The sea looked as if it came out of a postcard with its picturesque views and colourful boats. It almost felt like there was some kind of magic in the air when I came across a musician, who played an instrument I had not seen before. He was looking deep into the sea and played so peacefully. The man looked like an aed [prophet/seer], who just happened to be there. It looked almost too perfect to be real. As if he was supposed to be there at that time. The emotions I felt inspired me to write and that's how 'Notesheet From The Dawn Of The Light' was created."

[72] Natalie Nera states that she is, "not of a friend of 'back stories'", stating that, in her view, "having to explain my writing defies the object of the poem or story I have written. I believe all creative works live their own lives through participation of a reader, listener or a viewer who adds their own experiences or views, and processes them on a deep emotional level. I love the fact that what I write and what I intend to say may not be the same as the meaning my readers will attribute to my work.

"The poem 'Windowpane' arose from the isolation of the lockdown that forced us to confront ourselves, our own insecurities. The situation demanded some form of introspection from all of us. We normally don't have, or don't make time, to look at our past traumas. Instead, we tend to sweep them under the carpet and thus label them as a 'problem solved'.

"One such trauma is the subject of my poem: it addresses the issue of the loss of a child and the fact that there is a wall of silence surrounding the loss. You are supposed to move on and live your life but it is never quite possible. Just because it happens to many families around the world, to many people, it is not any easier and the pain never goes away."

[73] Helen Oliver tells us that the encounter at Brisbane Airport in 2018, described in her poem, 'Brisbane Airport – Encounter' (well before Covid fears), haunted her throughout her flight back to New Zealand and for days afterwards. "It epitomised the worst of officiousness," she writes, "in what is already quite a fraught situation (international airport procedures) – it could have been handled in a much gentler and different manner. While wanting to intervene, I felt helpless as I had no idea why the passenger was 'lost'; plus of course I was in a lengthy queue with a plane to catch."

[74] Helen Oliver describes, 'Clapotis', as a very early poem. "It's a kayaking image: feeling the force of big waves and their surge back from a rock face, *clapotis*, which can throw me off my kayak if I'm not wary – and the parallel I felt in my relationship, where my stronger partner could overwhelm me with the force of his reaction or argument."

[75] Helen Oliver was given a postcard of "glorious dark irises" in a writing exercise to write a haiku. "This led me," she tells us, to think of her mother, and she wrote this:

" 'Dark fragile beauty / memories of my mother / deep well of loss … love'.

"I recalled her love of flowers, her fervent belief that she could pray while tending her garden as well as in church (whereas my father felt we must go to church in person!) – I read a bit about the significance of irises … and this poem, 'Irises', emerged."

[76] Writing of her poem, 'Still My Restless Mind', Helen Oliver says, "In a busy life, juggling work, family, friends, issues and other commitments, it's easy for our attention to become splintered and fragmented, for us to feel restless and edgy. At such times, I turn to my tai chi practice, using breath to find inner stillness."

[77] The phrase, 'The Sad Limitations Of Love' caught the eye of Helen Oliver. "Like a magpie I noted it down – and in a time of emotional upheaval this poem almost wrote itself!"

[78] Rena Ong's poem, 'As we watch you walk away', was written, Rena writes, "as our son left Singapore to go to a new life in Australia. As we waved goodbye at the airport.

"It reflects the feeling we had as parents, desiring our child to be happy and fulfilled, to be the independent person he is meant to be, but this came with the sacrifice of 'letting go'.

"We had put in place all that was needed for him to walk his own path, but except for visits, despite our love for each other reaching distances, we can no longer hold him, physically protect him. We smile, as he must never feel guilty of chasing his dream, the one we encouraged him in, in the first place, but there is always a little shadow in our hearts until we meet up again, that is when the sun shines full bright. Though we would not have changed a thing, as his life is full, knowing he is happy makes it all worthwhile."

[79] Rena Ong's poem, 'Innocence' is one of her three poems in this anthology, which are dedicated to the work of Sydney Harpley, R.A., a British sculptor, three of whose bronze works are located in the Singapore Botanical Gardens. Rena explains, "What appealed to me personally was how naturally these 'children' were posed. It felt as if I had accidentally stumbled into their own garden as they were watering the flowers. The older child is probably around seven years old and the younger no more than four. This could be a snapshot taken by an adoring parent. As a work in bronze, their innocence as children is frozen forever in time."

[80] Rena Ong writes about her poem, 'Reminder'. "I live in Singapore and often walk in the Botanical Gardens, which is now a UNESCO heritage site. The poem, 'Girl on a hammock', was written on one of my walks as I admired the bronze artwork by British sculptor Sydney Harpley, R.A. 'Girl on a hammock' is one of three statues in the park by him of young women. I was struck by the lazy lounging and feeling of safety shown by the girl lying naked in her hammock under the

tropical sun, and also by the beauty of the gardens. I was also struck by the fact that, not far away, there was a simple staircase, called 'The Prisoner of War Steps', made from hundreds of bricks constructed by prisoners of war interned initially at the Selerang Barracks and Changi prison, which were later laid by Australian POWs in 1942. There was a stark contrast between the peace I was seeing under the same tropical sun, the same tropical plants, but totally different circumstances. One of peace and security, the other of endurance and cruelty.

"Some bricks have arrows carved in them, a sign to others they existed, and sadly now for some, their tombstones. 'Lest we Forget' is often quoted on the days of remembrance for all the soldiers who sacrificed their lives in the two World Wars and subsequent wars, and whose sacrifice we must always remember, no matter our opinion about war, or about the time that has gone by."

[81] Rena Ong writes, "Walking around the Botanical Gardens in Singapore is delightful, not only because of being in nature, learning about plants, but also because of the various sculptures which are dotted about the park. These include three bronze 'young girl' sculptures by Sydney Harpley, including the subject of my poem, 'Joy'. It depicts a young girl, probably around ten years old – but the age is irrelevant for this piece – as it depicts the sheer joy of allowing one's bicycle to go downhill (in this case a downward spiral of Eugenia bushes) and the momentary feeling of complete freedom. The hands on the handlebars are the only things which ground the girl. And who hasn't done as she is doing – knowing it is safe, as the gradient isn't too steep, and there is only oneself on the road – just lifted one's feet for a moment, letting the bicycle and gravity take over, feeling complete freedom?"

[82] Jun Pan explains that, 'A Free Verse Of Food' is, "a blended poem written in response to the proposed subject, 'Hunger', and against the background of the corona virus pandemic, during which – and especially at the beginning – people in many places of the world were relying on food delivery and were worried about food access.

"The poem was inspired by a random search of the phrase, 'food is' on Google. The resulting phrases/sentences were selected and arranged to create an interrelated 'blend' to represent what food is and is associated with. For instance, 'a four-letter word' corresponds to 'fuel', 'love' and 'life'. While 'my passion' forms a parallel to 'love', 'thy medicine' echoes 'medicine' in the first line. By using the archaic word 'thy' to introduce a modern (sometimes paranoid) thought about food, the end line creates an ironic contrast.

"The poem is also a 'blend' in the sense that it integrates different sayings about food in various languages and cultures. Each saying constitutes an interpretation of the previous line in a unique way, and is placed in round brackets to show this relationship. The original form/sound of the various sayings is retained in order to represent food *as it is*. I hope to bring readers a unique visual experience through this practice."

Asked to provide pronunciation advice, Dr Pan sent the following:
"民以食為天
man4 yi5 sik6 wai4 tin1

食べ物は口から入って
　　　体のどこを通るか
tabemono wa kuchi kara haitte
　　　karada no doko o tooru ka"

<u>Notes from Jun Pan</u>
"rén shì tiě fàn shì gāng": romanisation of a Chinese saying which literally means "people are iron and rice (food) is steel".
"民以食為天': Chinese saying which literally means, "people see food as important as sky/God". "食べ物は口から入って ／ 体のどこを通るか":
Japanese saying which literally translates as, "Is food what comes in by mouth and goes through the body?"
" (τροφή खाना cibus / gıda essen)": The word "food" in Greek, Hindi, Latin, Turkish, and German.

[83] Danny Dylan Poon explains that his poem, '27 August 2016', "was inspired by a conversation overheard from a dinner I had in a bistro/bookstore, a flashback of me travelling back home in a taxi late in the evening of 27 August 2016, together with a tiny bit of online conversation I had with my friend. The date used in the title is the day when I decided to go on with my literary expedition."

[84] Joanna Radwańska-Williams writes, "In the summer of 2019, I spent a couple of weeks on the pleasantly green campus of the University of Illinois at Champaign-Urbana, where I was delighted by several generations of hopping rabbits. The poem, 'Cottontails' is a meditation on their life. The 'scythe' is an evocation of medieval depictions/personifications of the figure of Death."

[85] Joanna Radwańska-Williams writes, "As the poem, 'Silhouette' describes, I was wandering in a happy and touristy mood through a

neighbourhood in Paris, where I took refuge in a lovely café, which served the best French onion soup I've ever had. At the table next to me, a grand old lady was seated, whom I surmised might have been a Japanese tourist, judging from the Japanese script hiragana she was enchantingly scribbling in what was probably her travel diary."

[86] Joanna Radwańska-Williams writes, "This mystical poem, 'The Medicine Wheel', came out of me after a conversation with my friend, the late Professor Robert N. St. Clair, who had done anthropological fieldwork on Native American cultures. In these indigenous cultures, the medicine wheel is symbolic of the circle of life."

[87] Colin Rampton describes his, 'Lines Of Nostalgia', as, "A lament to times gone by, before there were either political troubles or pandemics in Hong Kong.

"I arrived at the old Kai Tak airport with my wife and young family during late August 1989, for the beginning of a purportedly two-year teaching contract.

"It wasn't long before we had all fallen in love with the city. I never ceased to be fascinated by my new environment and its unique history.

"Twenty-eight years later, after numerous renewed contracts, it was time to retire and return to England. There will always be a part of Hong Kong within me, and I will be forever grateful for the numerous wonderful experiences I had while living there."

[88] Kerry Rawlinson writes of her poem, 'break/fast', "2020 has been a year of global tumult and political conflagration. We follow the news and social media mindlessly to see what the next worst thing is – which itself intensifies our self-indulgent rabbit holes. Then, one day, I'd had enough. It was as if my brain became nauseous. I felt overwhelmed, and needed my mind, as a stomach would, to be cleansed; to rise with daybreak and require only tea. I intended the poem to mimic a child's sing-song litany, taking its lead from the old wives' tale about breakfast, and interplayed media items with breakfast items and our seeming egocentric gluttony for, and slavish cultural propagation of, both."

[89] M. Ann Reed writes, "Praying with 13th c. Benedictine Hildegard of Bingen's prayer, I offer my translation from the Old German, 'God hugs you – Love's mystery encircles you, and you shine'. Initially, I offered this prayer for a father whose son had died, yet when I then offered this prayer for his son, both the father and I felt the tears

welling up and out, releasing the grief to realize the son's new beginning. A resulting condition of bliss accompanied me afterward, when, strangely enough, I sat before a window, drinking coffee and watching thousands of winged maple-seeds fall from many maple trees. Like the father's and my tears, were the falling winged seeds wooing new life? Juxtaposing the prayer and nature's experiences, I realized and related both to E. E. Cummings's mathematics of meiosis, the I-Ching, and David Bohm's quantum theory of implicate orders of reality that have yet to manifest."
<u>Notes from M. Ann Reed</u>
'one's not half two. It is two /are halves of one': from E. E. Cummings's poem, beginning, "one's not half two."
Bohm: Einstein's protégé, David Bohm, theorizes implicate and explicate orders of reality – orders twinned like winged-seeds.

[90] Vinni C Relwani describes her comment on, 'Clouds', as, "More of a humorous aside. This poem was crafted under the mistaken belief that a haiku comprised three lines, of 5, 12 and 5 syllables respectively. I later discovered the correct format of a traditional haiku, which still comprises three lines, but of 5, 7 and 5 syllables respectively. This poem (yes, poem, and not haiku!) still tickles, when I think on its origin. The content came about while day-dreaming, looking up at the clouds."

[91] Vinni C Relwani's poem, 'Hand in Hand', is dedicated to her parents. "This poem was inspired by the strength and grace I saw in them, after facing tragedy. They continue to inspire."
<u>Note from Vinni C Relwani</u>
For those unfamiliar, the first line of the poem references the Hindu wedding ceremony, which takes place around a sacred fire.

[92] Vinni C Relwani tells us that, "After a spontaneous meditative moment in the Singapore Botanic Gardens one morning, I was drawn to trying to capture the experience in words. 'Into the Garden' is a verbal expression of that very spiritual experience. To convey and further express the ethereal nature of the event, the poem is presented in italics."

[93] Vinni C Relwani's poem, 'LOL', "came about after observing a near-accident one day, as a pedestrian crossed a busy road while jabbing at her hand-phone, eyes glued to its screen instead of looking around her on the road. This became an all-too-familiar scene, and played heavily on my mind. Were they asking to become statistics? Did they not care

what might happen to them, to those around them, and the effects on their loved ones should the worst happen? Would they feel remorse, regret, in their final moments? What compelled them to lose themselves in their electronic devices instead of engaging appropriately – nay, necessarily – with their environment? The poem also incorporates a phenomenon of today's generation – something I have still to become accustomed to – the acronym; taking creative liberty in the exploration of this within the poem's lines."

[94] "During the height of covid-19, cowering in its wrath", Vinni C Relwani revisited a poem that, "was born of the feeling of near hopelessness, certainly helplessness – elements that became all-too-familiar again. 'The Angst Of It All' delves into the topics of bullying and abuse, verbal and emotional; and the toll it can take. It is left open-ended, almost as if in waiting for resolution … much as in the current climate."

[95] Vinni C Relwani asks, "How often do we allow, consciously or subconsciously, the authentic self to be seen? Whether introverted, cocooned, and wearing a mask for the world, or all-out sharing of every detail of one's life from the mundane to the spectacular, what should be the juxtaposition of both these states seems instead to show an almost complete overlap – one can be 'hidden', either way. What does it take to be seen through these façades? *Who* does it take, to see? And when it happens, it is rare and special indeed. The poem, 'To Be Seen, To Be Known, To Be Understood', is about one of those times…"

[96] In talking about his poem, Halil Suat Saraç first quotes Samuel Beckett:
"there's going to be a story, someone's going to try and tell a story. Yes, no more denials, all is false, there is no one, it's understood, there is nothing" "let us be dupes, dupes of every time and tense, until it's done, all past and done, and the voices cease, it's only voices."
—Samuel Beckett *textes pour rien* (Texts for Nothing).

Halil Suat Saraç then continues as follows: "'Faceted Bones Of Hunger' is fragmented – faceted as its title suggests. It depicts different states of hunger from several perspectives/voices. Hunger is analyzed (first stanza) from a newborn baby's perspective, the baby's initial reaction to coming to earth is anger. The poet suggests that leaving the womb is painful, it initiates hunger. Hunger is later analyzed from a god's perspective (first three lines of the second stanza) who, the poet's voice argues, is creating laws of the universe out of hunger. Hunger is later analyzed in a love scene between a 'he' and a 'she'. In the manner of a conversation (the rest of the second stanza) they discuss if their hunger, desire will ever ultimately be satisfied in the relationship, they question, discuss the possibility of an eternal satiety. The third stanza is a monologue by the main voice: 'he'. It repeats the points the poem makes this time presenting them to the 'she'. In the fourth stanza, 'he' addresses 'she' pleading hunger.

"Lastly, hunger is analyzed as the ultimate human condition. The poem ends in the shape of a prayer, the conclusion at which the main character arrives after his poetic inquiry into hunger. He has no choice but to embrace it, by doing so he refuses the Abrahamic religious consolation of an eternally satisfactory God or heaven. Gods and heavens are hungry, the poet is similarly hungry.

"The grammatical and capitalization 'errors', unusual cut and start of lines, overall the disorder in the format of the poem represent the mad mind of the voices and reigning of disorder that ultimately leads to the refusal of errorless Gods and heavens. The poem instead embraces life full of beautiful, hungry chaos."

[97] José Manuel Sevilla writes this about his poem, 'My City':
"This poem was written in and about Hong Kong just before the end in 2020 of the post-Handover régime, when the city was already drifting in turbulent waters. There is a longing for the lost and beloved city: – vibrant (people moving fast like birds), tolerant (no colours), open (no wall); a place of opportunities where new ventures and dreams were possible – hence the image from *My Darling Clementine*, one of the most touching final scenes in the history of cinema. The poet sees himself from the tram – a symbol of Hong Kong – as the improbable sheriff, Wyatt Earp, declaring Clementine Carter his love, before she decides to stay as a teacher and he leaves galloping on his horse with the promise of coming back. This was Hong Kong for me, a confession of true love and the promise of a happy future. However, that future was about to die (the storks do not stop anymore), as later events proved."
Note from José Manuel Sevilla
... "maybe because here the tourists are not for stones
nor to climb towers if there are no escalators...."
The above two lines refer to my observation that, "Tourists in Hong Kong are mainly mainlanders who come for shopping, and are not interested in anything cultural."

[98] José Manuel Sevilla writes this about his poem, 'Power'.

"This poem was written during the beginning of the pandemic in Wuhan and the first revelations of its spread to the rest of the world as a result of predictable, systemic mishandling.

"A bizarre and inconvenient power leads the narrator to discover a new pandemic and its Patient Zero but, as happened with Covid-19, he remained silent.

"Some of my real life observations appear throughout the poem: mortgages bind couples more than children; shameless corruption; women raised to smile all their life; the lines from Henley's famous, extraordinary poem, 'Invictus'. And two autobiographical notes: a quote from my own family doctor and my expulsion from the then francoist Spanish army which I had been forced to join."

Note from José Manuel Sevilla

"My use of 'Wella Farga' as the name of a mortgage is a joking reference to Wells Fargo bank, one of the biggest mortgage lenders."

[99] Of the poem, 'Hunger', Wesley Sims writes, "When I was a young teenager growing up in the rural south of the United States, a new family moved into our community. The mother had no husband in the home and no job outside the home or other visible means of support, e.g., no farm or animals, no products to sell. She had a teenaged daughter and two younger children. The family didn't have an automobile. I would sometimes see the daughter walking a mile or so along the highway to the only local market. I saw her a few times in the market getting groceries.

"Rumours circulated among the community about the variety of vehicles often seen parked at their house for a while. I didn't hear any other facts from adults I knew about the family's real situation, and I think few facts were known. I did hear some other young teens snickering about Fanny and her mother and singing a short uncomplimentary song they made up about her.

"As an adult with some years of maturity I developed more compassion for the mother and daughter and grew to be less judgmental about unfortunate people like them."

[100] Hayley Ann Solomon writes about her poem, 'On season's whim'. "This was written both as an emotional challenge and as a scholarly exercise. On an emotional level, I wished to evoke an intense hunger – a slow starvation of the soul, of the elements needed for love to survive and thrive.

"The poem is infused with nostalgia – what once was, certainly is no more – perhaps never <u>has</u> been.

"The last lines reveal the persona's reluctance to acknowledge this, but the insight to begin asking those hard questions.

> I hardly have the means or heart
> To chart the question why?

"Clearly, the persona has difficulty disentangling her emotions and creating the distance necessary for separation and healing.

> My freezing fingers follow him,
> but falter with my sigh.

"Here, psychological cold manifests in physical cold – clinging is wasted – this uselessness is acknowledged not explicitly, but implicitly, with a soundless sigh.

"The poem was written as an interesting technical challenge, bringing into play its secondary motivation of scholarly exercise.

"It is written in alternating iambic tetrameter (abab rhyme scheme) and trimeter (ccc) followed by one line of trimeter with a peppering of cross rhymes (cxb).

"In my habitual style, I make use of sound-play through alliteration, assonance and consonance.

"The theme of hunger was brought into play. I thought it might be interesting to interpret hunger on the metaphysical rather than the physical plane."

[101] Hayley Ann Solomon writes that, 'Tell me and I will try' is a poem that probably doesn't need a backstory. "It is inspired by world hunger, world poverty, world anguish and a recognition of the unfairness of a life that is bountiful for some and drudgery for others.

"It is written from the perspective of one who is entitled, and strikes an ironic note from the first stanza, juxtaposing self-oriented discomfort and guilt and the genuine issues arising from true despair, disempowerment and hopelessness.

"It touches on human nature, and on avarice undermining the dire concerns of the genuinely downtrodden.

> Eyes blinded by greed and a million
> words of cunning pouring from honeyed lips.

"It touches on guilt, and the emotional resonance of voiding unpleasantness by seeking solace in ignorance.

"There is good will in this poem, but also a recognition that good will is not enough.

"The last line, 'tell me and I will try' almost embeds the hopelessness.

"'Trying' is simply not good enough, and 'succeeding' does not seem viable.

"Both poet and reader know there is nothing to 'tell' – the impoverished will remain voiceless, the genuine well-wisher disempowered. It is a conundrum too great to bridge, with diminishment the only outcome of insight.

"For a subject as intense as this, the poem has abandoned traditional end rhyme, with its comforting rhythms. It prefers harsh starkness, allowing only the occasional half rhyme and alliteration to provide poetic cadence.

"Thus, the more subtle, 'following my footsteps with *stares* of / unspoken *despair...*' precedes alliteration such as in, 'wordless eyes' and 'whispers of humanity'. The words, 'wordless' and 'whispers' are, of course, juxtaposed with the hint of an oxymoron to create dissonance through structure.

"The poem ends on a hopeful note, but that hope is so pathetically parsed – 'I will try'– that it resonates with the despair of the entire passage, lending sad truth to the damning lines, "the certainty in strained eyes / that I will do nothing /and there is no point in / talking."

"The poem's intention is to reveal the true poignancy of hunger – hunger that is physical, spiritual and unabated."

[102] Robin Susanto gives this background to the poem, 'Buddha In Stone (2)'.

"Borobudur is a Mahayana Buddhist temple in Indonesia, built in the ninth century. In our time, as the country's Buddhist population has shrunk to a tiny minority, the temple functions more as a monument and tourist attraction.

"I remember going to Borobudur as part of a field trip in middle school. It was almost a standard part of the curriculum for schools in the surrounding area, and also for those from further away, as long as they could afford the trip. I also visited the temple on family road trips. But it left no impression on me. Maybe I was too young. Maybe that's what being a tourist means. I remember the sights, the heat, but then a few years – or a few days – later, it's all gone. The souvenirs I brought home lie mute, indistinguishable among all the mute trinkets in the apartment.

"It was not until many, many years later, after I had immigrated to Canada, that I returned to Borobudur. I made a point of not taking pictures. I wanted simply to be present, and to be conscious of my presence in that space so heavy with human history. I didn't want to be distracted by the busyness of taking souvenirs. I didn't want trinkets.

"It was a hot day. In the lower half of the temple, you can take shelter in the shadows of the walled corridors. But as you climb up to the upper levels, the walls disappear. It's just you, the sun above, the fields below, the mountains in the distance, and Buddha statues arranged in circles on platforms stacked like the layers of a wedding cake. Each of the Buddha statues is supposed to be housed inside a stupa – as a symbol of something I can no longer recall from my middle school lesson. But some of the stupas have crumbled and the Buddha can been seen in his signature pose: the erect spine, the perfectly resting head, the hands in a *mudra*.

"And then there is the gaze.

"The eyelids are lowered. You can't quite tell if the eyes are open or closed, but you can tell there is this soft unrelenting gaze, a gaze that does not stare, but does not shy away either, a gaze that does not so much look as behold. And what it beholds – the black bricks underfoot, the mountains in the distance, me in my sweat-drenched T-shirt – these things somehow feel it, and become more conscious of themselves by means of this contact.

"'This is creation,' I thought.

"Maybe this is what happens between the still-life painter and the bowl of fruit he paints. In that beholding at a distance, in that commitment of the eye and refrain of the hands, both the seer and the seen become created – and come to life.

"I ended up staying the whole day. I wanted to try out this new way of seeing – try it out on the sparse line of trees the field below, the line of food stalls, the school children on their field trips, the other tourists, everything. I thought of the world's problems: the decline of nature, the oppression of the weak. They still beset me. I was still invested. I was still powerless. But on that day being powerless did not mean fretting; it didn't mean worrying. Thinking is a kind of seeing. If you know how to see, you know how to think. The sun was setting. It was beautiful. I stuck to my decision not to take pictures. But I did scribble some lines in my notebook, something about a way of seeing a bird without catching it out of flight.

"I am not a Buddhist. But as I left I did make a bow before a Buddha in stone."

[103] Robin Susanto writes this about his poem, 'Winter Deciduous'. "Nothing is more barren, the dark, leafless deciduous trees of winter, barely living twigs, thin and spindly. They look almost 2D, like some

gnarled fingers lifted in silhouettes against the flat, grey sky. I remember snapping pictures of them, almost instinctively. I would point my camera up, framing the pictures without showing any ground so these dark figures would look like one of those dried plants, pressed against the pages of the sky. It was during my first winter in Canada, after immigrating from the tropics. I was having a hard time, lonely and isolated. Maybe I found in these trees some kind of kinship. If I did, I wasn't conscious of it.

"It wasn't until many years later that 'Winter Deciduous', the poem, showed up. I had made a home in my new country, though the journey toward a true arrival continues still, homeward and landward. Much of the journey involved walking among trees, in summer and in winter too. I knew I would not arrive until I knew the land, and was known by the land. I wanted to know the trees, not so much in terms of their scientific classification, natural history, or trivia or tidbits, which I could find from an app. What I really wanted was to experience their presence, and how, sometimes, something in me, something ancient and true and ineffable, would change shape to fit itself to that presence, just as my body would bend and curve to settle onto a bench. What I really wanted was an encounter.

"It was during one of these winter walks, in the evening, that the grace of these trees spoke: a thing that answers the cold not by bundling up like I do, but by stripping itself bare – and thus prove the cold wrong. 'Death itself is alive.' 'Nothing else can be so sharply both tree of life, and crucifixes of the field.' And as if in response, that ineffable something in me became words. I jotted them down in my scrap-book. By the following spring the poem was finished, which was a record time for me."

[104] Luisa Ternau describes her poem, 'Birthday Song', as, "a light-hearted poem about celebrating birthdays. A reflection on the ups and downs of everyday life during the year leads to a final expression of gratitude on the day of one's birth."

[105] Luisa Ternau's poem, 'Hunger', is, "a reflection on hunger manifested by a patient who must fast before surgery. Words of encouragement clash with the feeling of hunger and the inability to restrain it."

[106] Luisa Ternau says this about, 'Not Forgotten'. "In this poem dormant feelings awake to portray a state of mind created by a mysterious attraction to someone in the past. Something that still fascinates and saddens the protagonist of the poem. The lost address of

the place that should have safe-guarded such precious feelings shows the apparent unattainability of this love."

[107] Luisa Ternau's, 'The Christmas Scarf' was written, "after taking my class of young children to a local rest home for disadvantaged old people. Each pupil was to sing and dance in front of one elderly person sitting along with others in rows. Both children and the elderly residents were encouraged to participate in the song and dance. Children did not seem to be too affected by the elderly faces' expressions ranging from sheer joy and even participation with movements of the arms, when possible, to indifference. Most teachers later admitted that they had found it difficult to hide their feelings of distress. The poem ponders what the gift of a scarf from the hands of a young stranger could mean to those elderly people."

[108] Luisa Ternau's poem, 'To My Mother', "is a reflection on my mother's earthly life and possible development in life beyond death. The inspiration draws abundantly on the blue colour of her eyes, which earned her many compliments during her lifetime."

[109] Non vedro' piu' gli occhi bellissimi di mia madre
non li vedro' nell'atmosfera profana di questa terra
Mia madre,
un angelo che Dio ha voluto terreno
per un po', per il tempo di una vita

Madre, i tuoi occhi hanno affascinato
questo mondo pieno di colore
coprente la cenere da cui veniamo
A cui torniamo
quando
L'angelo arriva con la tromba
E Dio chiama
 squilllandi sopra ogni voce
di questo mondo, di questa foresta
dove la tenebra sembra regnare.
Madre, rivedro' i tuoi occhi
nei non-ti-scordar-di-me
e nei laghetti alpini
abbacinanti di luce
nelle gole ghiacciate
che urlano di bellezza

Per via dei tuoi occhi celesti
Ti vedro' nell' azzurro del cielo assolato
Tu che sei stata il pittore
del mio ritratto piu' vero

Madre,
E' dolce pensarti che la notte
vicino alla luna mi guardi
Cosi' io ti vedo, io che ti credo gia' in Paradiso
mentre in compagnia degli angeli sorridi

[110] Writing of his poem, 'Dreaming of Food', Edward Tiesse says, "In my family, meals – especially for the holidays – were important. All the grandparents, aunts, uncles and cousins gathered together and shared food, recent family events and hopes for the future. So, I find it curious that I don't dream of these gatherings. For my work, I travel extensively and getting home to have a meal with my family is very important. I often dream of trying to get home. Also, I was influenced by *The Hungry Ear* a collection of poems about food edited by Kevin Young."

[111] Bibiana writes, "I had returned to Hong Kong from my trip to Britain when I wrote this piece. I was in quarantine and was re-visiting Milton's *Paradise Lost* which I had studied in the UK, and the following lines caught my attention.

" '... Now conscience wakes despair
That slumbered, wakes the bitter memory
Of what he was, what is, and what must be
Worse: of worse deeds worse sufferings must ensue.
Sometimes towards Eden which now in his view
Lay pleasant his grieved look he fixes sad,
Sometimes towards Heav'n and the full-blazing sun
Which now sat high in his meridian tower.'
—Book Four, *Paradise Lost,* John Milton

"Impressed by Milton's compassionate narrative, I tried writing a few lines in iambic pentameter and decided to entertain myself with a challenge during quarantine. When I pondered the fate of Lucifer and the lovers in Eden, I could not help but empathize with Lucifer. The work clearly departs from Milton's original and is a recreation based on personal experience and beliefs."

<u>Notes from Bibiana Tsang</u>
"Common": alludes to Common Aphrodite in Plato's *Symposium*.
"Heavn'ly Love": alludes to Heavenly Aphrodite in Plato's *Symposium*.
"Love of Beauty, good and ill alike": alludes to Keats's idea of Beauty.
See Richard Harter Fogle, 'Beauty and Truth: John Middleton Murry
On Keats.' *The D.H. Lawrence Review*, Vol. 2, No. 1, 1969, pp. 68-75.)
"figure": generic reference to the shapes of everything whether they are
tangible or not, the essence of the figure is that it embodies the
"Beauty" of the "good and ill alike".
"*his* hate for *he*": Satan's hate for himself

[112] Bibiana Tsang writes, "In January 2020, I arrived in the UK for an
exchange semester at a local university. I was shopping for some
supplies at Tesco with a friend. Since it was my first day – the day of
my arrival – all I had was several fifty-pound notes. My interaction
with the cashier later became an inspiration for this piece.

"It was a very difficult time, to be so far away from my family in
a foreign city, which did not seem happy to have me. During my stay in
the UK, I thought a lot about my identity as a Hong Kong girl and
reflected upon the way my friends and I use the Chinese and English
languages. There is a word in Chinese, 根源, which means one's 'root'
and origin. I reflected, and realized that, as a middle-class girl,
proficiency in English is a crucial indicator of future success. It is only
natural to be away from one's roots as one ascends the social ladder,
similar to the case with a tree. As a tree grows taller day by day, the
crown eventually departs from the roots when it soars into the sky."

[113] Roger Uren, 'Hunger For Peace Of Mind'
<u>Note</u> "grate": *sic*.

[114] Writing from Badajoz, Spain, Rod Usher tells us this about his
poem, 'Desert Island Words'. "Desert Island Discs is a radio
programme started by the BBC back in 1942. Well-known people
choose a very limited number of songs or pieces of music they would
take if stuck on a desert island (It's assumed there would be a player of
some sort).

"This poem suggests Desert Island Words, where the choices are
even more vast.

"Many languages offer words that sound a lot better than their
English counterparts, as in Murrumbidgee, from my native Australia. I
speak Spanish and some Italian so I looked for words that sound better
in those languages than they do in English. I think the Italian *aquilone*
flies off the tongue a lot better than does *kite*.

"I had a bit of fun with delicious *camembert*, also with the strict 17 syllables of Japan's *haiku*.

"The end of the poem offers a twist, if you like a trick, where I use *sine qua non*, which in English, via Latin, is *without which nothing*, usually a term used by lawyers, but which in the poem refers to people's need for people, though it might take being lost on a desert island for this to hit home."

[115] Peter Coe Verbica writes, "'A Line of Expectations' is the result of a writing exercise given at a Creativity Unlimited workshop by Kaecey McCormick, Cupertino's Poet Laureate *emerita*. We were asked to utilize a refrain as a poetic device and to enhance impact.

"The craggy landscape, lead character, villagers, livestock and narrator in 'A Line of Expectations' intertwine as participants.

"I imagine the setting to be either in Ireland or Scotland.

"It's my intent that the licentiousness is viewed from the perspective of a forgiving and matter-of-fact Creator. While necessity keeps the lead character in her trade at present, there is the tantalizing hope of freedom in her not-too-distant future."

[116] Peter Coe Verbica writes, "'A Typical Modern Chilean Day' is an informal, conversational ode in honor of Pablo Neruda; the reader may catch tongue-and-cheek references to him throughout the poem (his hometown, his epic ways of romancing women, political persuasion, and predilection for wearing a suit, as well as the image of Chile in the 'map of perspiration' on his shirt). The introduction is a nod to the current pandemic. The reference to 'petty dictators' rhymes with our current political unrest. While 'magical realism' is largely absent in the poem, I was ever conscious of the Latin American affection for this tradition (i.e., having Neruda alive even though he had passed away years' prior). The piece hearkens to another poem which I wrote, entitled, 'A Six Course Breakfast' (featured in *Left at the Gate and Other Poems*)."
Editors' Note: the frogs and flies mentioned in stanza 6 are an allusion to the plagues of Egypt.

[117] Sarah Vetter tell us, "The act of writing my poem, 'I thought I told them for you', was inspired by the prompt, *mingled voices*, though the memory it reconstructs is much older. I wanted back a particular moment, but from the perspective of someone else, someone I loved very much (and write to remember). It happened when we needed to leave a house party before anyone knew he was there; despite his anxious state, he was uncharacteristically calm. Scores of years later, I

still remember the soft and detached way he apologized as I climbed
out a window and scaled the brick-walled building side, him in tow."
Note
"Abject and abscess": *sic*.

[118] Renee Wade explains that her poem, 'Whaea', is, "a dedication to
New Zealand Prime Minister, Jacinda Arden. I chose to use Te Reo
language to signify our nation as a whole, to honour our privilege in
being able to tap into Maori culture.

"Jacinda is like the mother (Whaea) of our country, showing us
her love and passion for New Zealand. She has demonstrated great
leadership qualities through trying times, including terrorist attacks,
and the covid-19 pandemic. Her positive outlook, intelligence, and
common sense unite our people. Jacinda Arden has become a great
female leader, who will be a role model for future generations. She is in
the right place to lead our country."
Notes from Renee Wade
English translation of Maori words:
Whaea: Mother, aunty, woman teacher (Jacinda Adern New Zealand
Prime minister)
Wahine: Woman
Aotearoa: New Zealand, land of the long white cloud
Waka: Water transportation, boat, ship, canoe
tangata whenua: People of the land, Maori
pakeha: White New Zealander
Kai: Food
Aroha: Love, Jacinda's daughter's name
Waiata: Song
Te rangatira: Princess
Taonga: Treasured gift, sacred treasure/possession

[119] Victoria Walvis writes, "'Eating for One' came out of a writing
workshop I did with a couple of friends, in which we each took an
object and wrote a poem inspired by that object. I picked a tin of
sardines – I happen to eat them a lot when I am lazy and can't be
bothered cooking for one. The tin struck me as an apt metaphor for
someone independent, self-contained, and yet packed with emotion!"

[120] Victoria Walvis writes, "'It is Spider Season' was inspired by a hike
from Mui Wo to Pui O [Mui Wo and Pui O are villages on Lantau, an
island which is part of Hong Kong territory – Ed.], in August when the
spiders were rife, and by a story told me by a stranger on the same hike
about the Cultural Revolution in China – he drew a comparison

between the gruesome story, told in the poem, and the way in which female spiders eat their babies. All of this, and the overpowering heat, made me feel queasy; it was a relief to arrive back in Mui Wo.”

[121] Victoria Walvis writes, “I wrote ‘The Harbour Swimmer’ when I was feeling a little homesick on a walk from Tsim Sha Tsui to Whampoa. At the Tai Wan Shan waterfront, where there are often locals swimming in the harbour (I have since swum there myself!), I paused to watch a swimmer. Watching the swimmer during the heat of June, I had the strange sensation of feeling quite distant from everything and everyone around me, more like the swimmer than myself.”

[122] <u>Note from Bruce Arlen Wasserman</u>
apresurándose, no: hurrying, no
el idioma: language
y nada me alejaría de la alegría: and nothing would keep me from joy

[123] Writing about his poem, ‘After the Storm and the Flood’, George Watt says, “There are flood and deluge myths in almost every culture. While Noah’s tale is the best known in the Christian West, there are other similar tales to be found around the world, like the great flood Prayala in the Hindu canon, and Plato’s record of Zeus who punishes the unworthy with a catastrophic deluge. This poem takes a whimsical, definitely surreal view of the drowned victim who has maintained his talents of observation. His first-hand account as a victim of a contemporary deluge does not seem to express any desire to return to his former life on land, or to the person waiting on the surface for his reappearance. This loved one waiting for him was obviously sufficiently righteous to avoid inclusion in the cataclysm in the first place. It is, of course, a nonsense poem, but I have been intrigued by his seemingly off-hand acceptance of his fate, and the notion that there is something of discovery in any new sphere of existence.”

[124] Of his poem, ‘An Embarrassment of Pleasure’, George Watt writes, “There are some joyous, brief moments in life where a completely unrelated set of sights, smells and sounds seems to converge; they belong together in a brief, almost perfect unity that does quite make sense. In this poem there are sounds of a man praying in a foreign tongue, the noise of unseen children playing in the distance, the quiet soft light of early evening, and the singular gift of flowers left by someone for strangers. Famously both Wordsworth and Coleridge felt that a poem was the ideal vehicle for capturing these fleeting moments

and so awarding them a kind of permanence. But it is not their work which was behind my writing of this poem, it was Robert Frost in 'The Tuft of Flowers'. Early in the poem the persona labours alone in a field bewailing his isolation, but he later experiences a moment of epiphany when a butterfly leads his eye to a 'leaping tongue of bloom the [former reaper's] scythe had spared.' On my daily walk by the River Torrens which runs through Adelaide, some kind soul had left an old drum filled with camellias, gifts for those passing by. It brought to mind the Frost work, and resulted in the poem now presented."

[125] Writing of his poem, 'Blackbirds of Cooper Place', George Watt says, "In my view, the hardest of poems to write convincingly are elegies – to get the right balance between overt statement and suggestive image, between emotional indulgence and aesthetic control, between the single lived experience and the desire to find a universal relevance that can appeal to any reader. This elegy, written for my mother's memorial service but never delivered, was no exception. In Adelaide where I live, the blackbirds' singing heralds the coming of spring, and they continue in the early morning and at sunset through that season into summer. In a country like Australia where birds tend to screech, gurgle, squawk, and laugh hysterically, by contrast the piping of the blackbird presents as especially musical. Behind this poem is the rich suggestibility of the following quote from Virginia Woolf in *To the Lighthouse*: 'And all the lives we ever lived and all the lives to be are full of trees and changing leaves.' And, I would add, the creatures in them. If anything lies behind my poem and can claim inspiration for it, it is Woolf's pitch for something so much bigger than any mere individual life, something to which we all belong, alive or dead."

[126] George Watt explains that his "simple poem", 'Empty', "retells one of my early memories, one that remains surprisingly vivid many, many decades later. It was the first day of school to which I happily went, armed with my new leather satchel. I found myself alone in the sports' changing-room with its rows of hooks, benches and lockers. What I was doing there, and who placed me there I have no idea. I wasn't unhappy to be waiting there, just somewhat bored. All I had was my empty bag that sat on my lap. The momentous event of that first day was undoing the heavy brass buckles, listening to the creaking sound of the thick, hard leather straps, then looking into its emptiness, and sensing that all sorts of things unknown, but terribly important, were going to find their way in. The importance of these unknown things demanded reverence, so I didn't want anyone else looking into the bag and 'seeing' them. They were mine, and mine alone."

[127] Elizabeth (Libby) Wong writes that her poem, 'To Hunger for Righteousness', is, "inspired by a combination of Christian faith and Chinese culture", as she explains.

"1) Christian faith

"The title itself is inspired by a biblical quotation, "Blessed are those who hunger and thirst after righteousness, for they shall be filled." The Gospel according to Saint Matthew, chapter 5, verses 3-6, King James' Version of the Christian Bible.

"As for the three verses of the poem itself, the spirit of love and courage runs through them. This is inspired by the Second Epistle to Timothy, chapter 1, verse 7, which reads, 'God has not given us a spirit of fear but of love and power and soundness of mind.'

"2) Chinese culture

"In parallel, running through the three verses of the poem is the theme of overcoming the pangs of hunger. In Chinese culture, there is the following time-honoured saying:

吃得苦中苦
方為人上人

The meaning of the above Chinese saying is similar to the western saying, 'No Pain No Gain'.

"At a personal level, I have experienced real hunger, having survived from a childhood where I experienced the real pangs of hunger, suffered during the Chinese war years. To me, hunger is real and I know what it feels like.

"The poem, therefore, is an amalgamation of the East and West, the personal with the universal, blending together variations of the spirit of endurance with the concept of humanity."

[128] Writing of the poem, 'Asylum in happy meals', Wing Chit Yung explains that, "the 'Mcrefugee' problem is prevalent in Hong Kong, which has numerous 24-hour fast food shops. These restaurants offer a relatively safe place to rest for poor people who are unable to pay the sky-high rents of the city, and an alternative to the cramped and usually hazardous subdivided flats. The poem dives into the fact that these 'refugees' have to situate themselves in an environment filled with sights and smells of food while they themselves are often hungry."

[129] Wing Chit Yung explains that the poem, 'Infection control', "is inspired by my own experiences in the medical laboratory, and safety measures implemented during the COVID-19 pandemic. In Hong

Kong, medical staff who take care of coronavirus patients are part of the 'dirty team'."

130 Wing Chit Yung tells us that, 'Voices of rain' is, "imagining the sounds that rain resembles in the political context of Hong Kong." She explains, "Hong Kong has been in a state of political unrest since June 2019, and there are several references in the poem to the protests, such as allusions to weapons and tactics, and the looming CCP."

SOME POETRY AND POETRY COLLECTIONS
Published by Proverse Hong Kong

Alphabet, by Andrew S. Guthrie. 2015.

Astra and Sebastian, by L.W. Illsley. 2011.

Bliss of Bewilderment, by Birgit Bunzel Linder. 2017.

The Burning Lake, by Jonathan Locke Hart. 2016.

Celestial Promise, by Hayley Ann Solomon. 2017.

Chasing light, by Patricia Glinton Meicholas. 2013.

China suite and other poems, by Gillian Bickley. 2009.

Epochal Reckonings, by J.P. Linstroth. 2020.

For the record and other poems of Hong Kong,
by Gillian Bickley. 2003.

Frida Kahlo's cry and other poems,
by Laura Solomon. 2015.

Grandfather's Robin, by Gillian Bickey. 2019.

Heart to Heart: Poems, by Patty Ho. 2010.

Home, away, elsewhere, by Vaughan Rapatahana. 2011.

Hong Kong: Growing Pains, by Jonathan Ng. 2020.

Immortelle and bhandaaraa poems,
by Lelawattee Manoo-Rahming. 2011.

In vitro, by Laura Solomon. 2nd ed. 2014.

Irreverent poems for pretentious people,
by Henrik Hoeg. 2016.

The layers between (essays and poems),
by Celia Claase. 2015.

Of leaves & ashes, by Patty Ho. 2016.

Life Lines, by Shahilla Shariff. 2011.

Mingled voices: the international Proverse Poetry Prize anthology 2016, edited by Gillian and Verner Bickley. 2017.

Mingled voices 2: the international Proverse Poetry Prize anthology 2017, edited by Gillian and Verner Bickley. 2018.

Mingled voices 3: the international Proverse Poetry Prize anthology 2018, edited by Gillian and Verner Bickley. 2019.

Mingled voices 4: the international Proverse Poetry Prize anthology 2019, edited by Gillian and Verner Bickley. 2020.

Moving house and other poems from Hong Kong,
by Gillian Bickley. 2005.

Over the Years: Selected Collected Poems, 1972-2015,
by Gillian Bickley. 2017.

Painting the borrowed house: poems,
by Kate Rogers. 2008.

Perceptions, by Gillian Bickley. 2012.

Poems from the Wilderness, by Jack Mayer. 2020.

Rain on the pacific coast, by Elbert Siu Ping Lee. 2013.

refrain, by Jason S. Polley. 2010.

Savage Charm, by Ahmed Elbeshlawy. 2019.

Shadow play, by James Norcliffe. 2012.

Shadows in deferment, by Birgit Bunzel Linder. 2013.

Shifting sands, by Deepa Vanjani. 2016.

Sightings: a collection of poetry, with an essay, 'communicating poems', by Gillian Bickley. 2007.

Smoked pearl: poems of Hong Kong and beyond, by Akin Jeje (Akinsola Olufemi Jeje). 2010.

Of symbols misused, by Mary-Jane Newton. 2011.

The Hummingbird Sometimes Flies Backwards, by D.J. Hamilton. 2019.

The Year of the Apparitions, by José Manuel Sevilla. 2020.

Unlocking, by Mary-Jane Newton. March 2014.

Violet, by Carolina Ilica. March 2019.

Wonder, lust & itchy feet, by Sally Dellow. 2011.

www.ingramcontent.com/pod-product-compliance
Lightning Source LLC
Chambersburg PA
CBHW070819170726
48000CB00019B/1466